Cedric & Friends DAD JOKES

Patrick Holden

© 2020 Patrick Holden

First published in the United Kingdom in 2020 by
The Cloister House Press
ISBN 978-1-909465-95-4

Welcome

"Done well, the single panel joke cartoon (gag) is a self-contained piece of comedy. In today's age of short attention span, cartoons hopefully amuse the reader with an instant hit. I trust my reader(s) will take time at least to flip through the examples on offer here."
Patrick Holden

Patrick Holden is an avid collector of original cartoon art and has been a Trustee of the Cartoon Museum in London for many years. Inspired by his favourite gags, he has now taken up pen and brush to craft his own cartoons. His work has been published in various magazines and shown at The Shrewsbury Cartoon Festival Exhibition (and on more than a few Christmas cards).

Patrick's other publications include books on Dog Training & Behaviour, Dog Agility, Footpaths, Local History and most recently Limericks.

"Very funny, Patrick has a great sense of humour. I thoroughly recommend it".
Anita O'Brien
Director/Curator of The Cartoon Museum

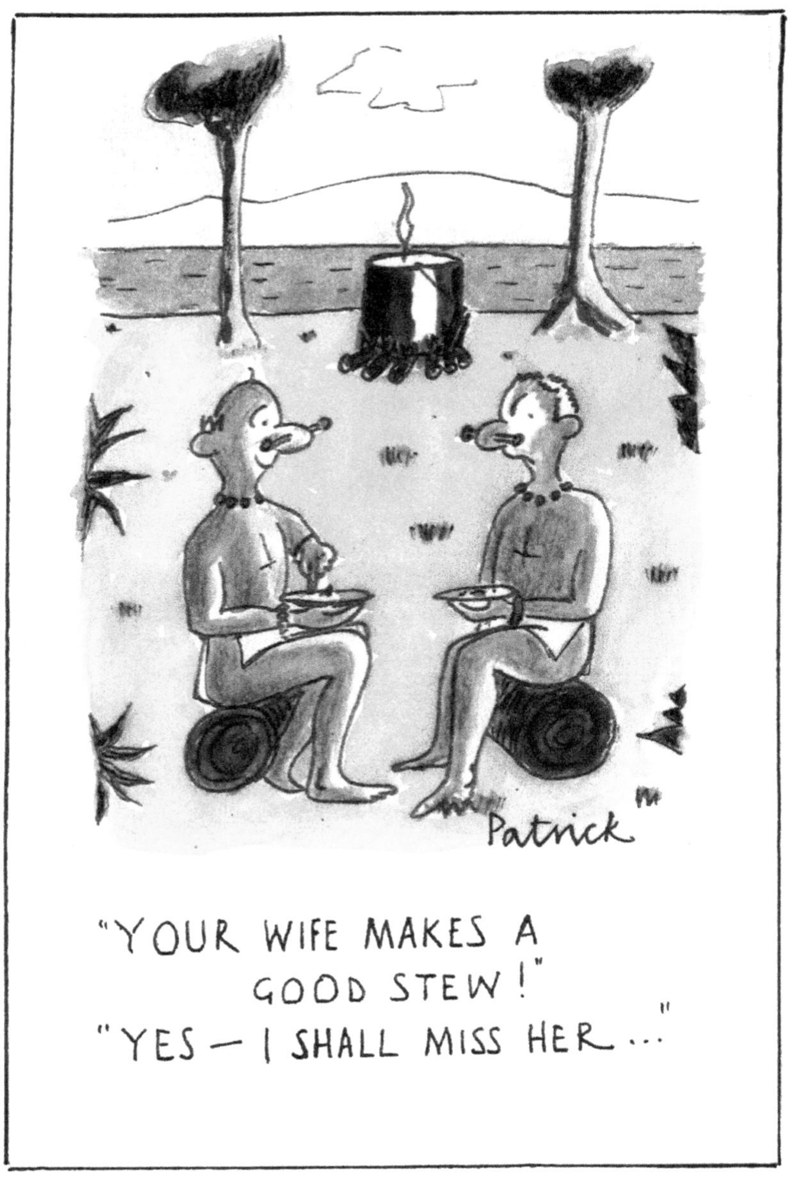
Patrick

"YOUR WIFE MAKES A GOOD STEW!"
"YES — I SHALL MISS HER..."

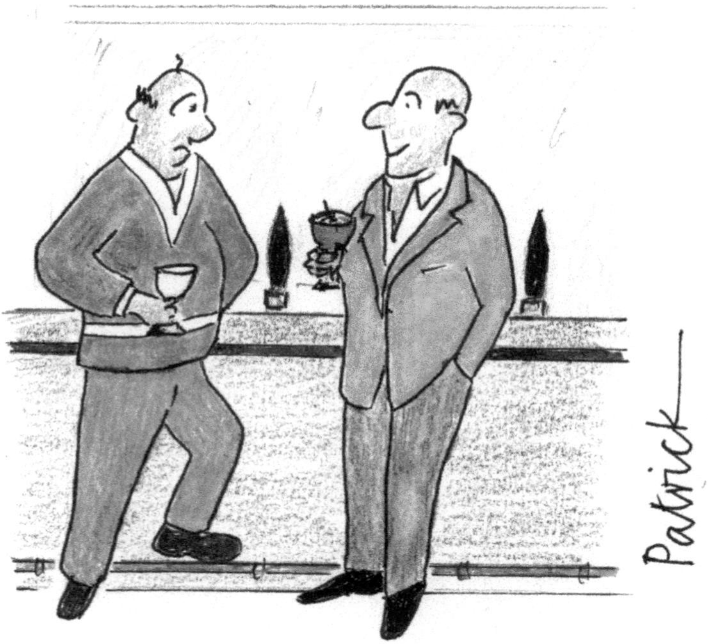
Patrick

MY EX-WIFE WAS A GOOD HOUSE KEEPER
- AFTER THE DIVORCE, SHE KEPT THE HOUSE!

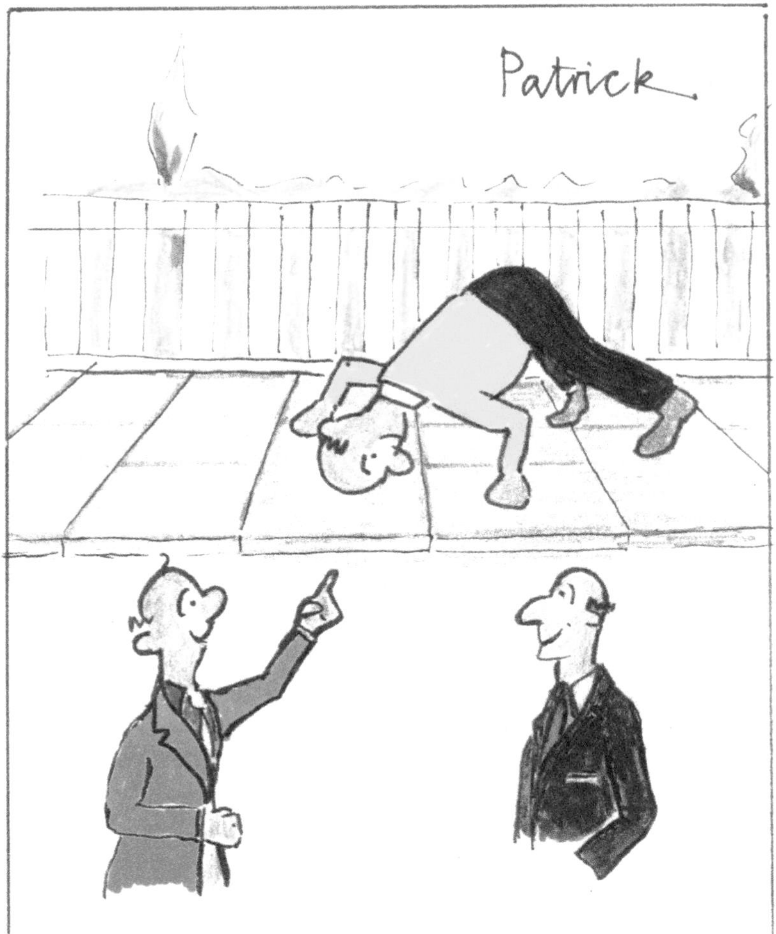
Patrick

" HE'S WELL INFORMED - HE KEEPS HIS EAR CLOSE TO THE GROUND!"

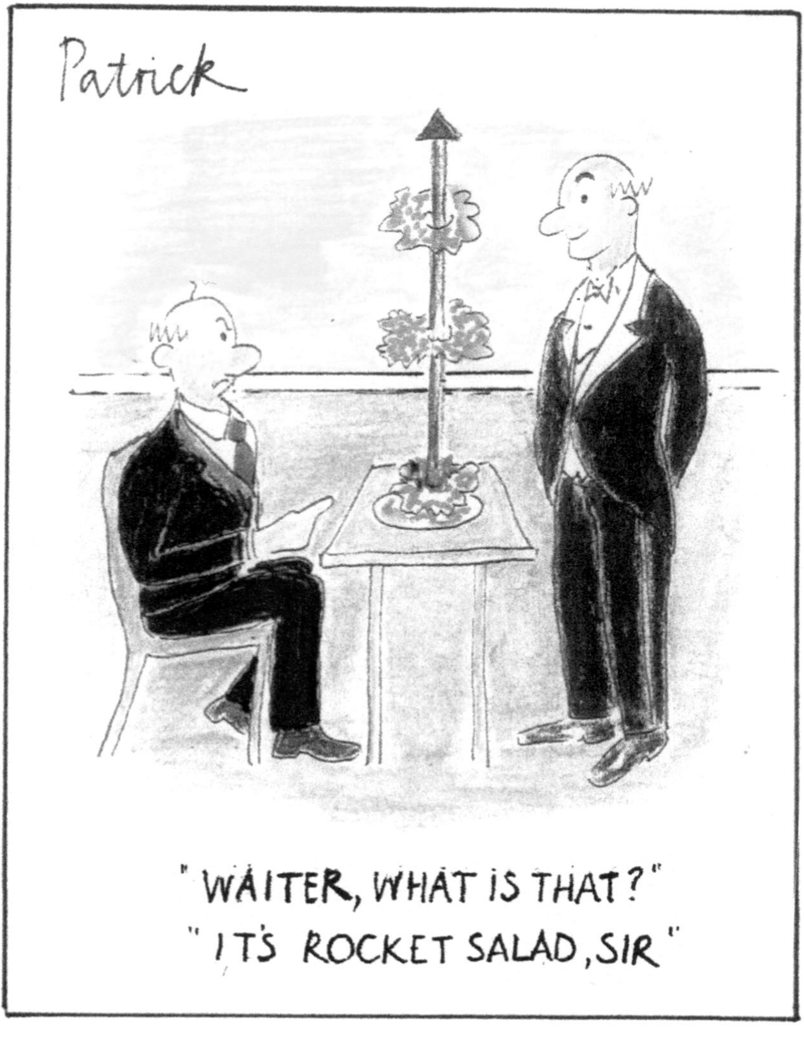
Patrick

"WAITER, WHAT IS THAT?"
"IT'S ROCKET SALAD, SIR"

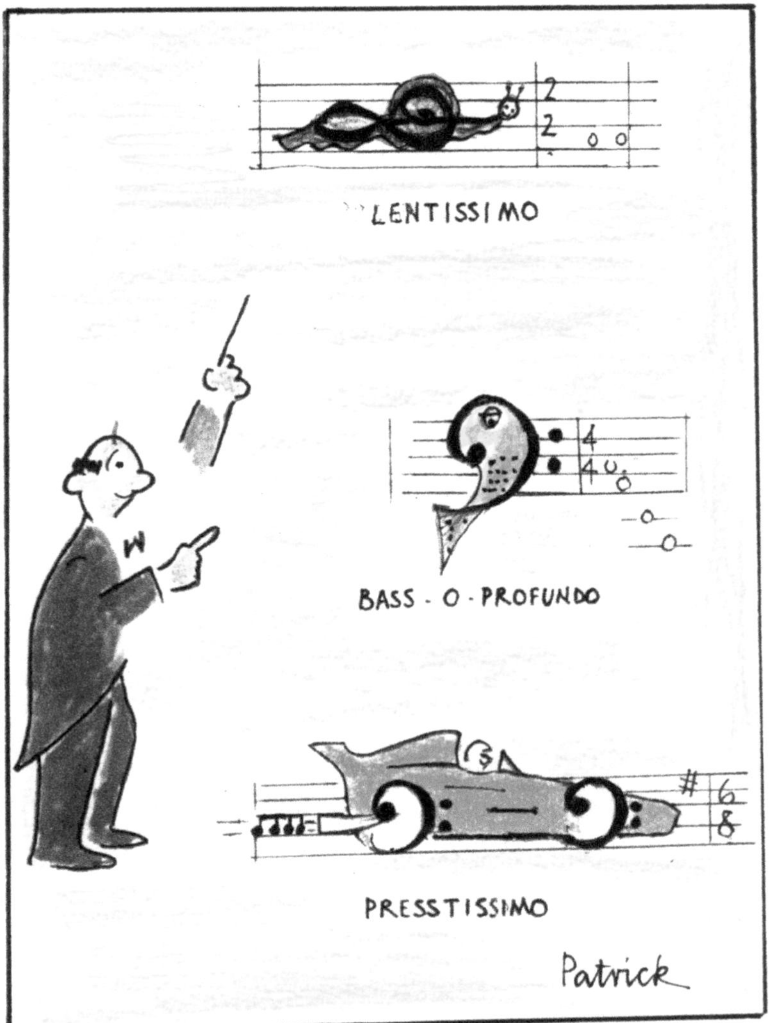
LENTISSIMO
BASS - O - PROFUNDO
PRESSTISSIMO
Patrick

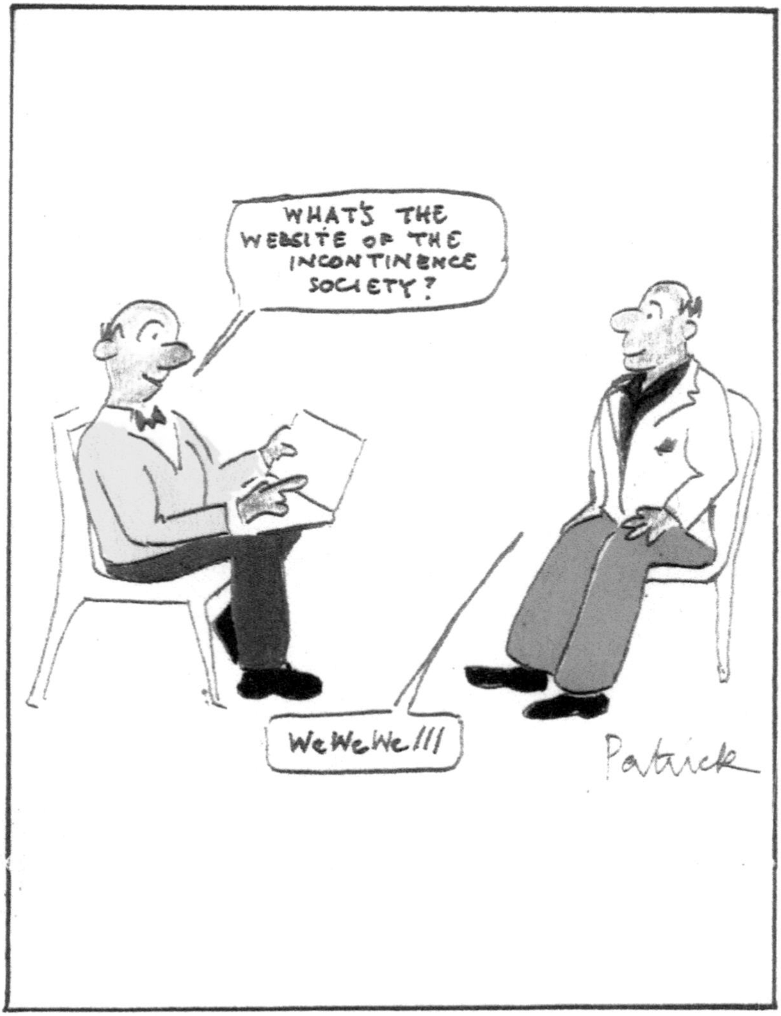
WHAT'S THE WEBSITE OF THE INCONTINENCE SOCIETY?
WeWeWe///
Patrick

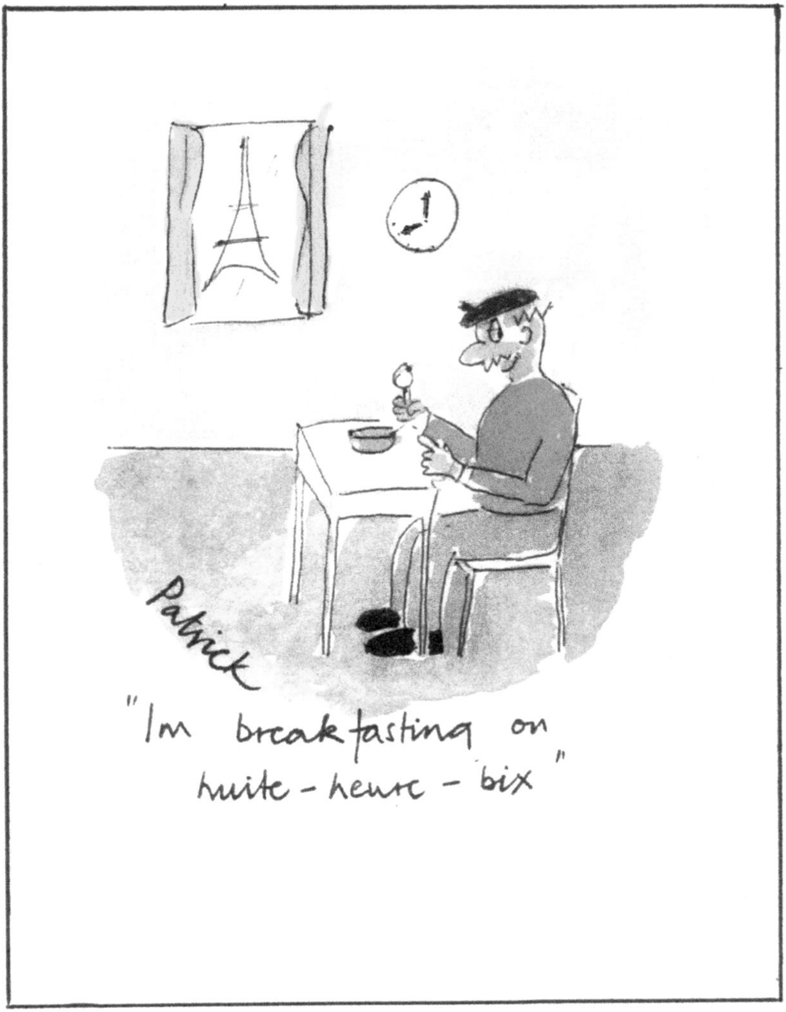
Patrick
"I'm breakfasting on huite-heure-bix"

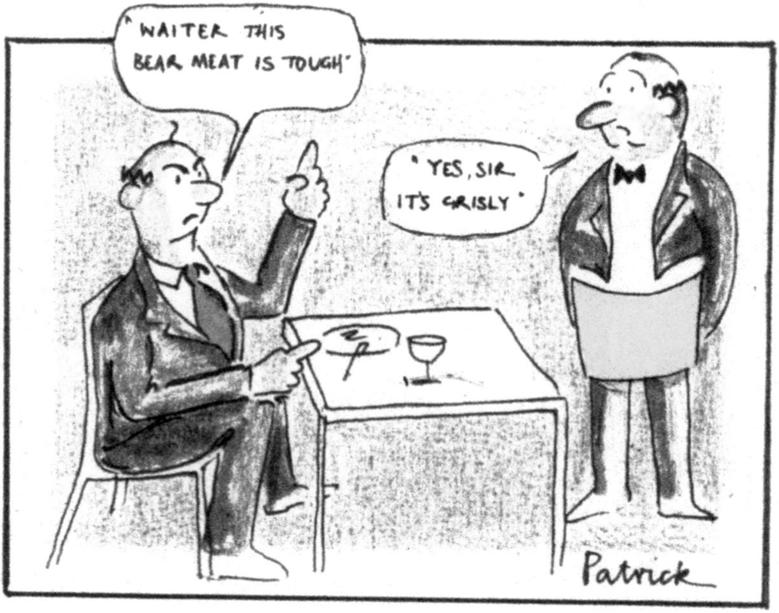
'WAITER THIS BEAR MEAT IS TOUGH'
'YES, SIR IT'S GRISLY'
Patrick

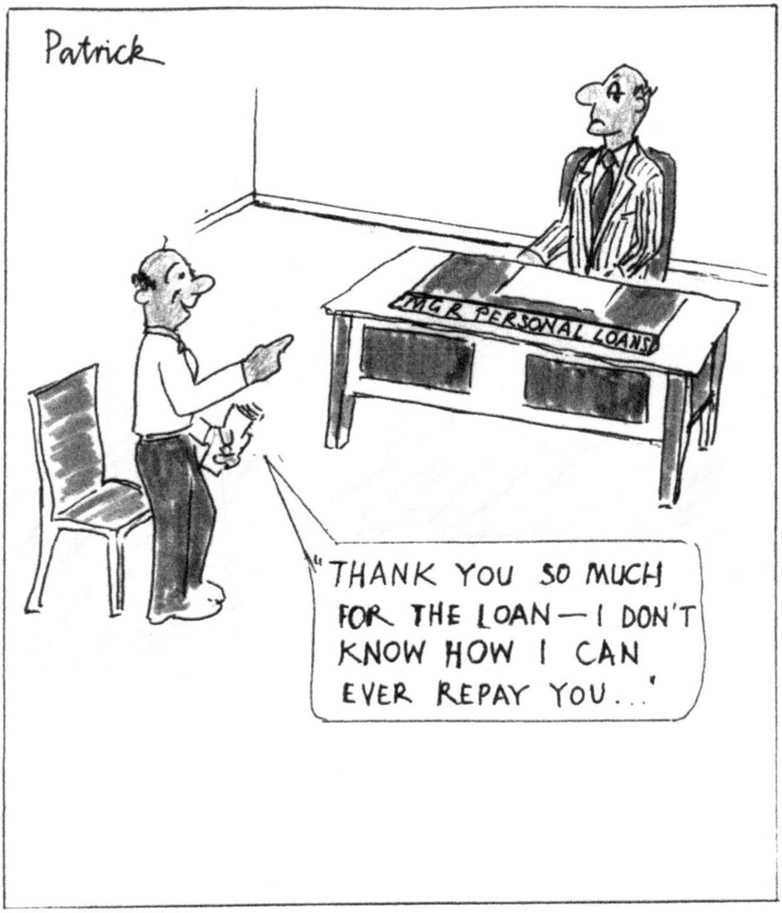
Patrick
MGR PERSONAL LOANS
"THANK YOU SO MUCH FOR THE LOAN — I DON'T KNOW HOW I CAN EVER REPAY YOU..."

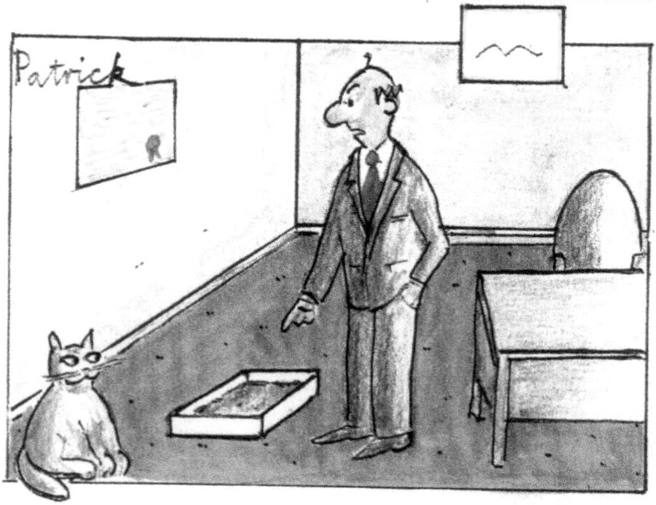
Patrick

"NEVER EVER, THINK OUTSIDE THE BOX...

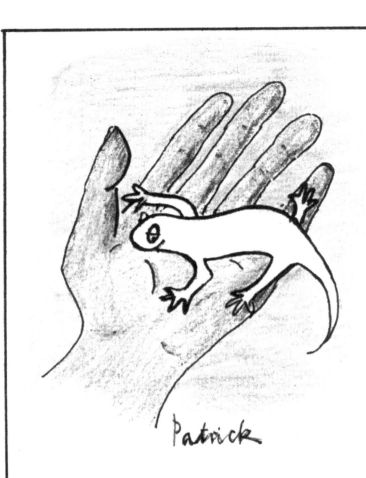

Patrick

"WHY DO I CALL HIM TINY ? "
" 'COS HE'S MY NEWT"

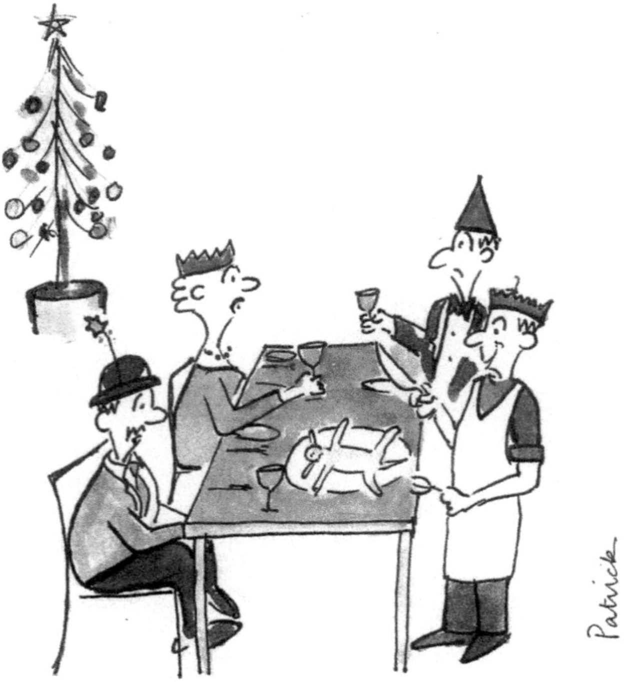
Patrick

"WE'RE HAVING
A PUPPY JUST FOR CHRISTMAS.."

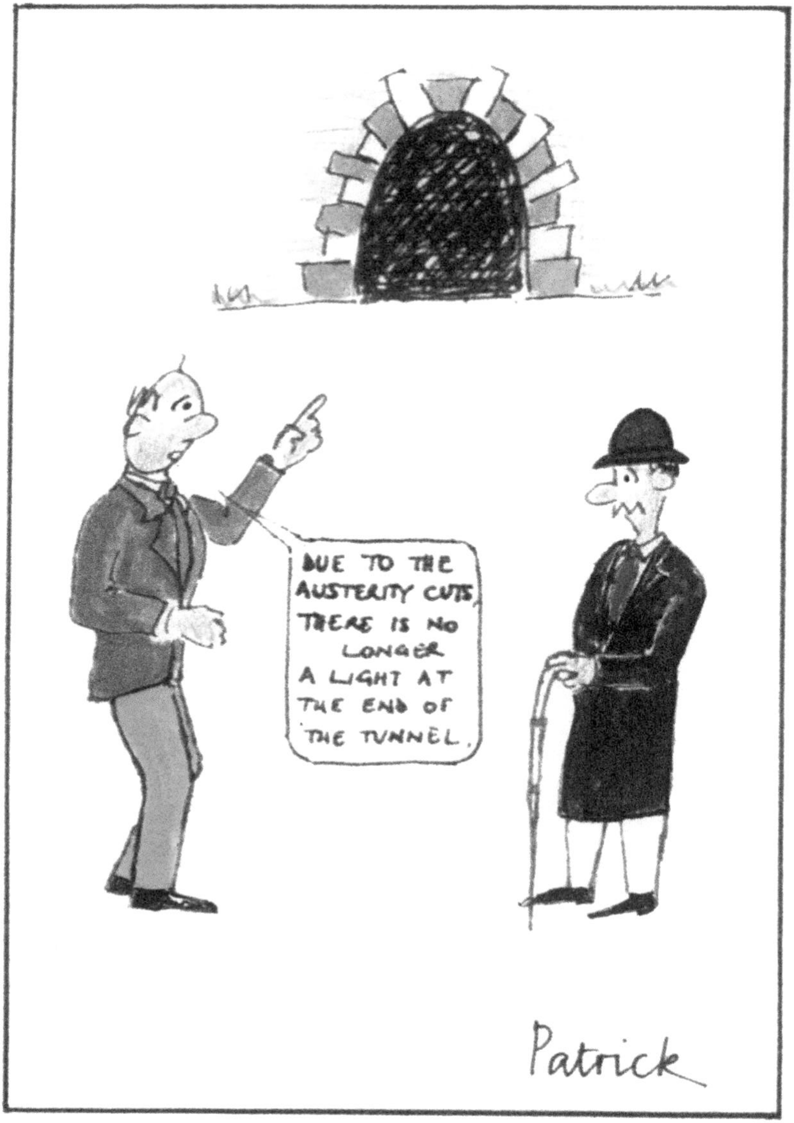
DUE TO THE AUSTERITY CUTS, THERE IS NO LONGER A LIGHT AT THE END OF THE TUNNEL.
Patrick

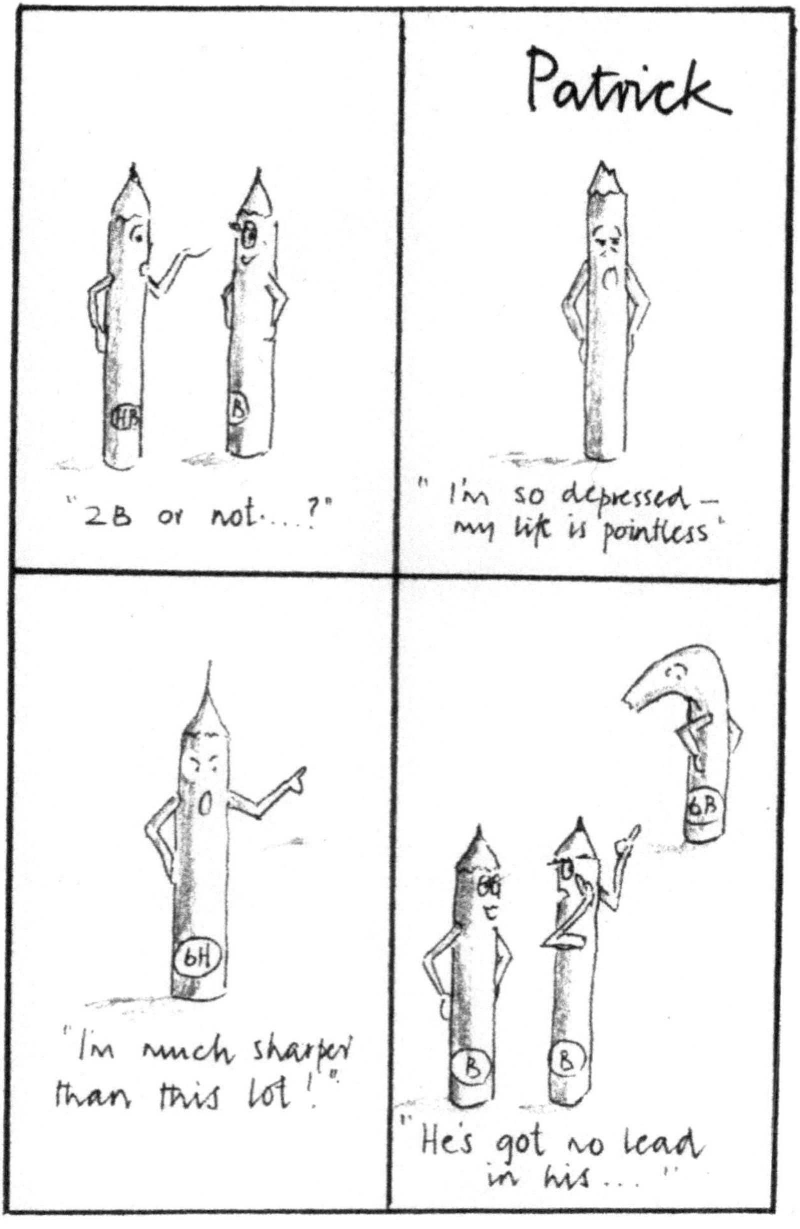
Patrick
HB
B
"2B or not...?"
"I'm so depressed – my life is pointless"
6H
"I'm much sharper than this lot!"
6B
B
B
"He's got no lead in his..."

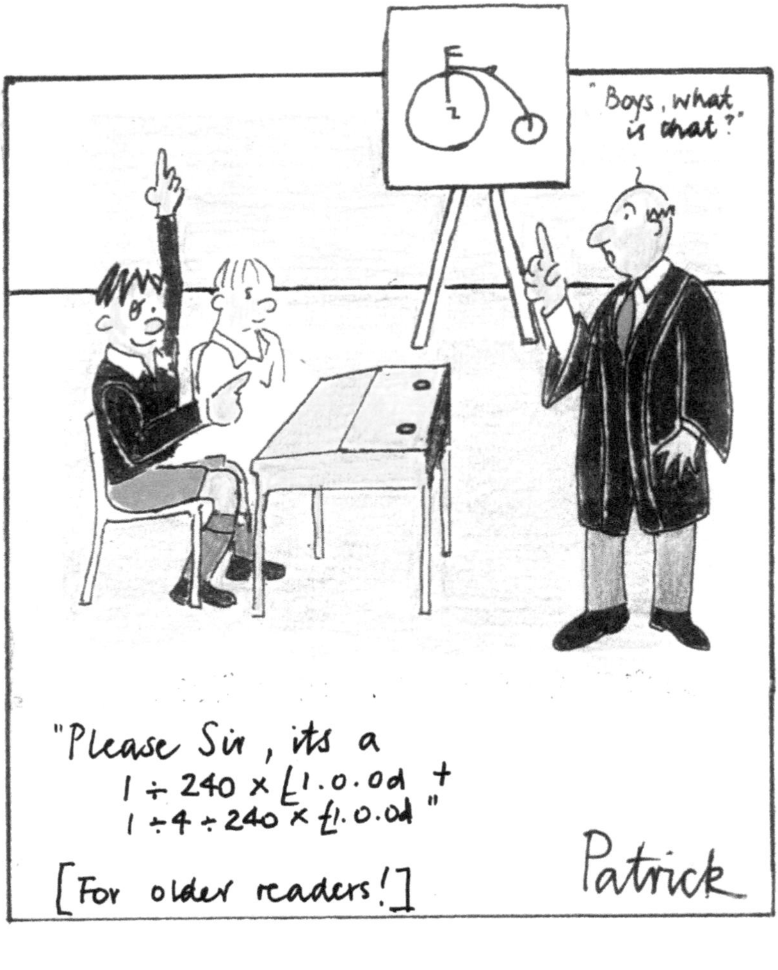
"Boys, what is that?"
"Please Sir, its a
1 ÷ 240 × £1.0.0d +
1 ÷ 4 ÷ 240 × £1.0.0d"
[For older readers!]
Patrick

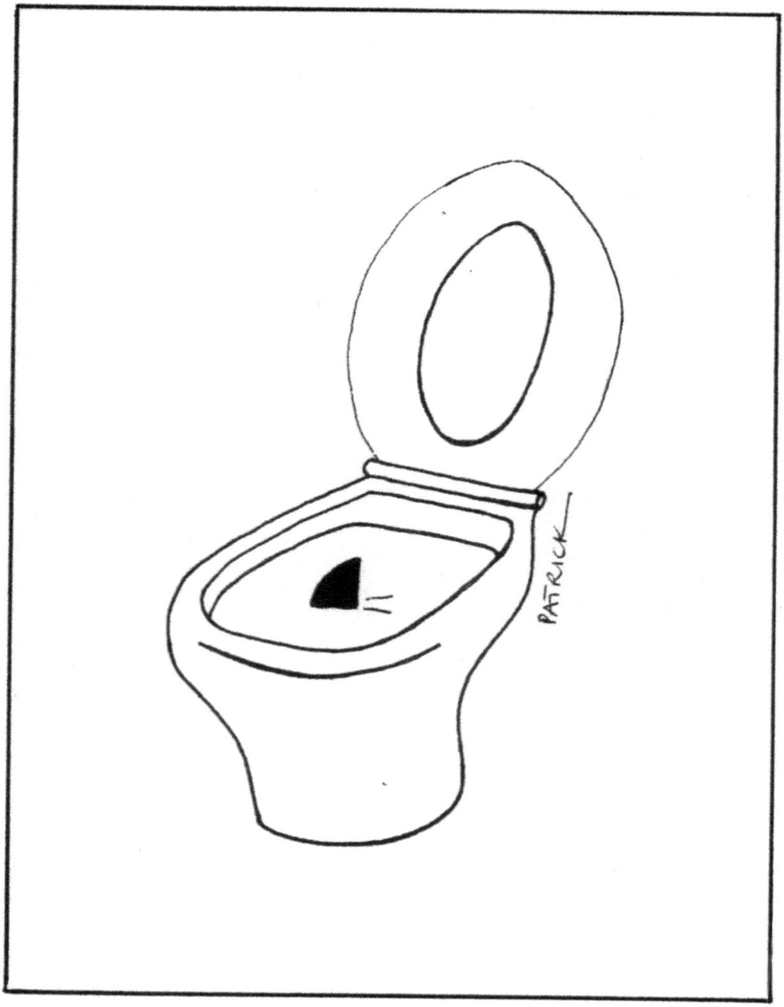
PATRICK

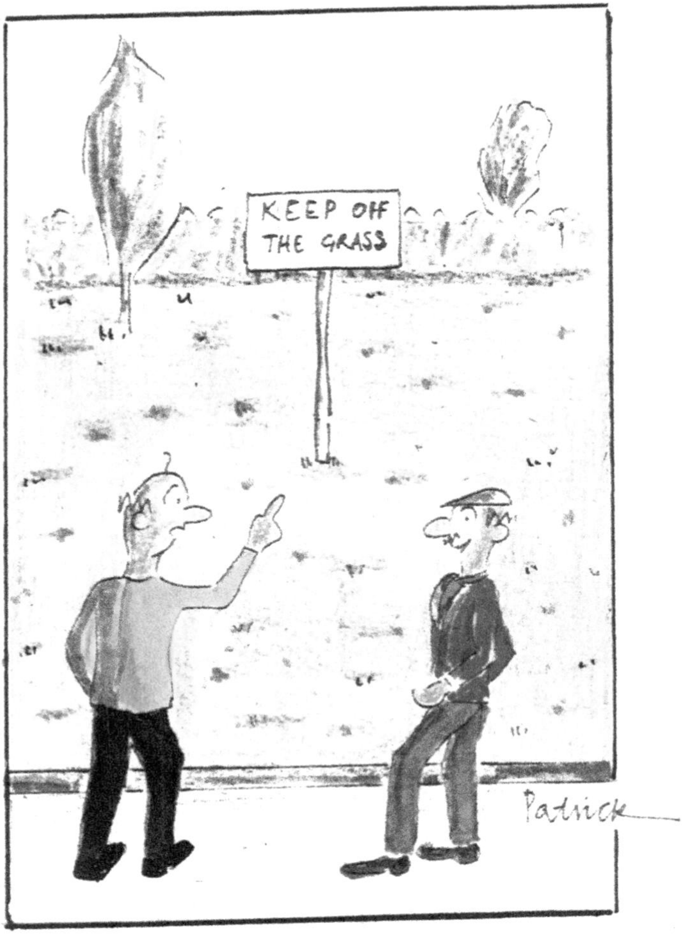
KEEP OFF
THE GRASS
Patrick

"SO, HOW DID THAT SIGN GET THERE?"

Patrick

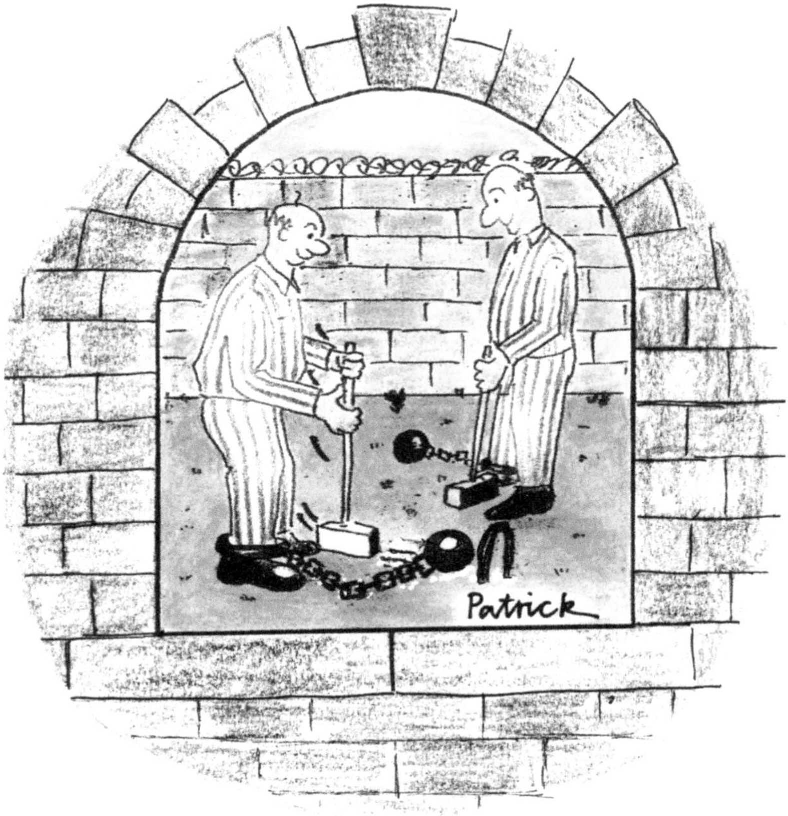
Patrick

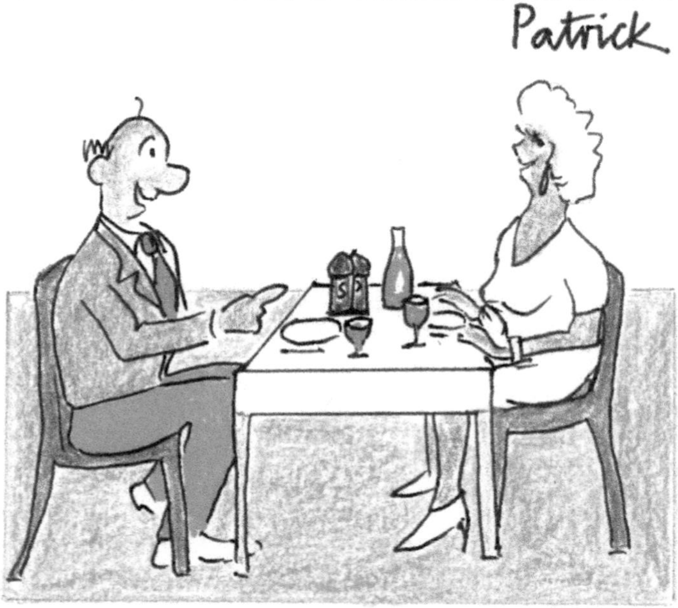
Patrick
S P

"I PRACTISE SAFE EATING –
I ALWAYS USE CONDIMENTS"

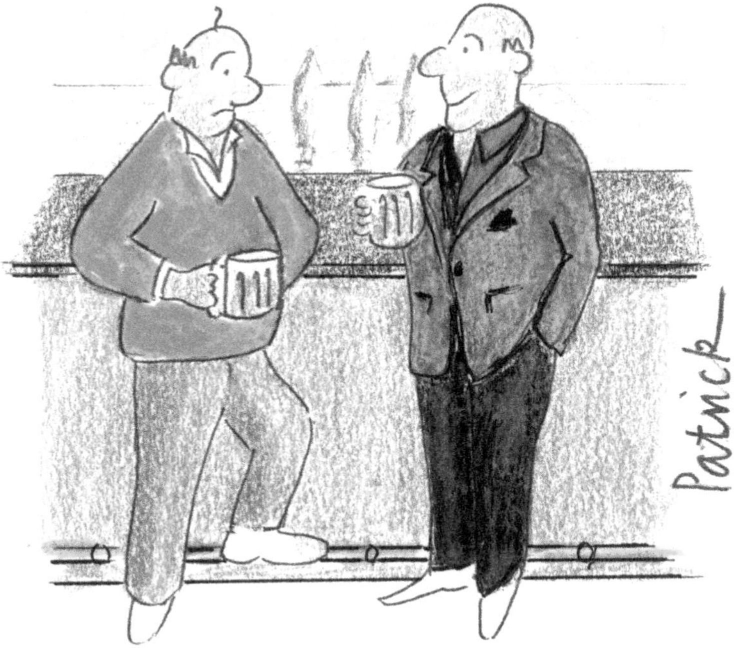
Patrick

" BOB HOPE WAS RIGHT
– WHEN HE SAID 'MIDDLE AGE
IS WHEN YOUR AGE STARTS TO
SHOW AROUND YOUR MIDDLE' "

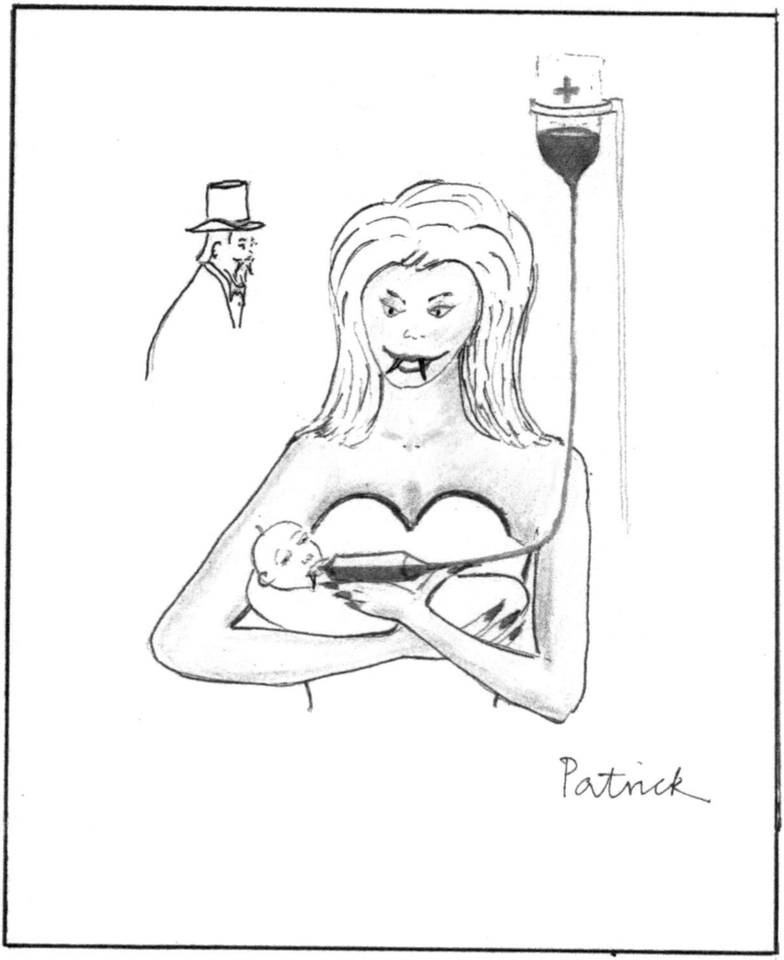
Patrick

"WHY DO YOU CALL YOUR DOG 'HANDYMAN'?"

"BECAUSE HE DOES LITTLE JOBS AROUND THE HOUSE"

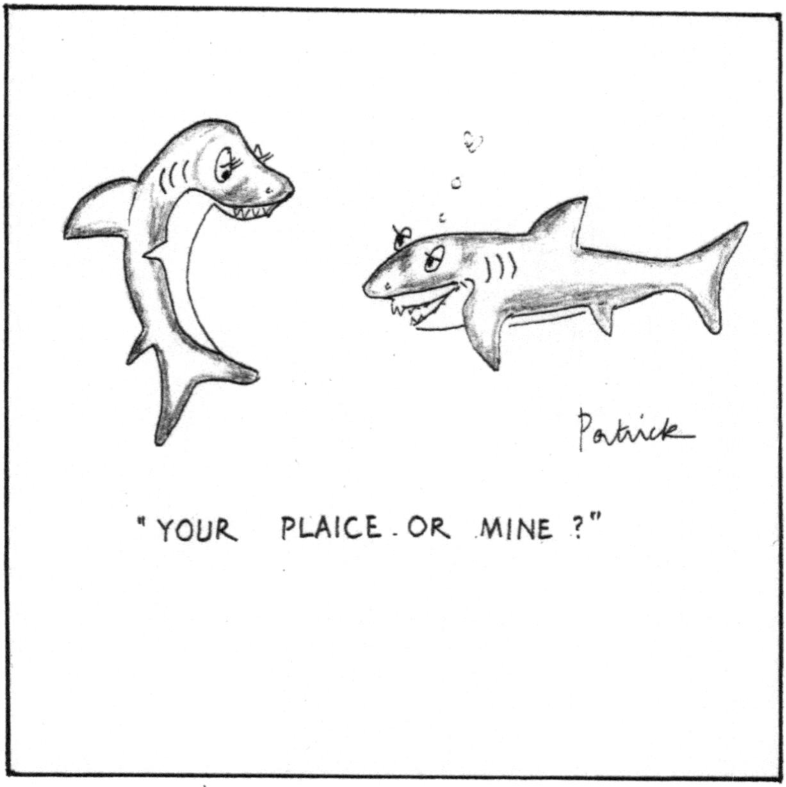
Patrick
"YOUR PLAICE OR MINE ?"

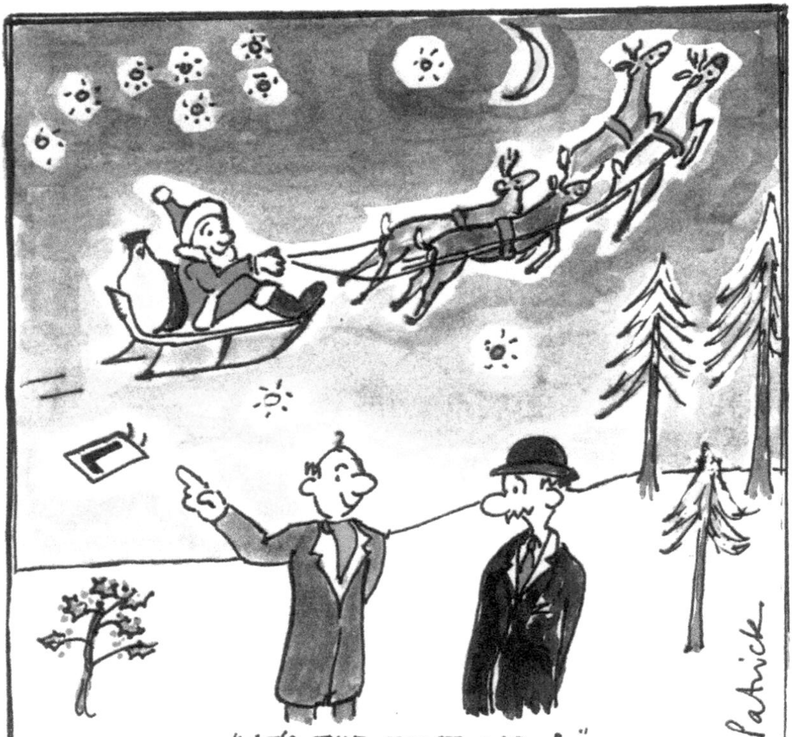
Patrick

"IT'S THE FIRST NO-L"

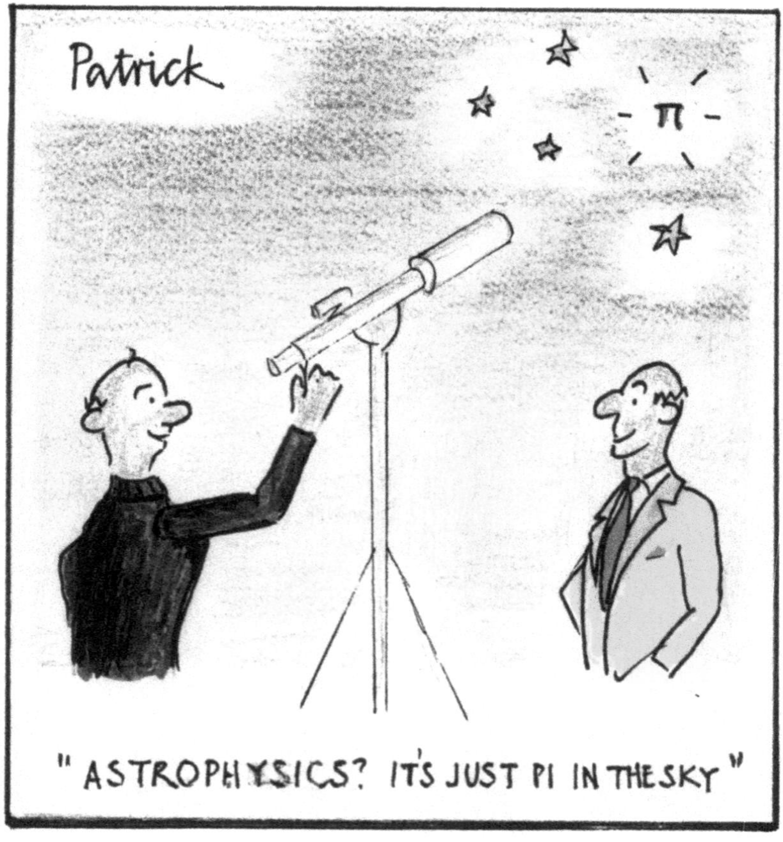
Patrick
π

"ASTROPHYSICS? IT'S JUST PI IN THE SKY"

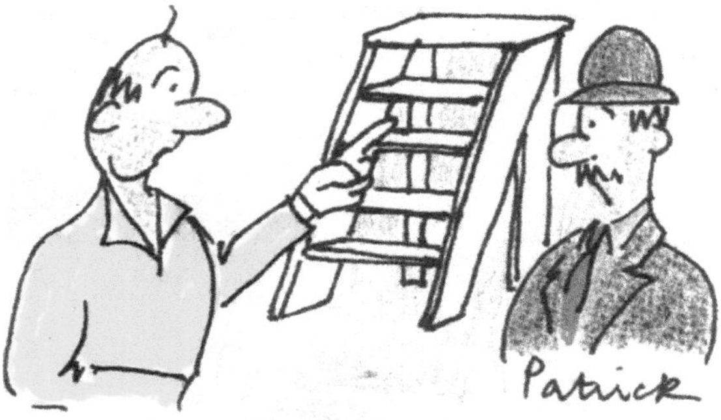
Patrick

That's only my stepladder — I never knew my real ladder.

OLD JOKE, UPDATED

"WAITER, THERE'S A FLY IN MY SOUP!"

"YES SIR, PLEASE DON'T WAVE IT ABOUT—
THEY'LL ALL WANT ONE."

Patrick

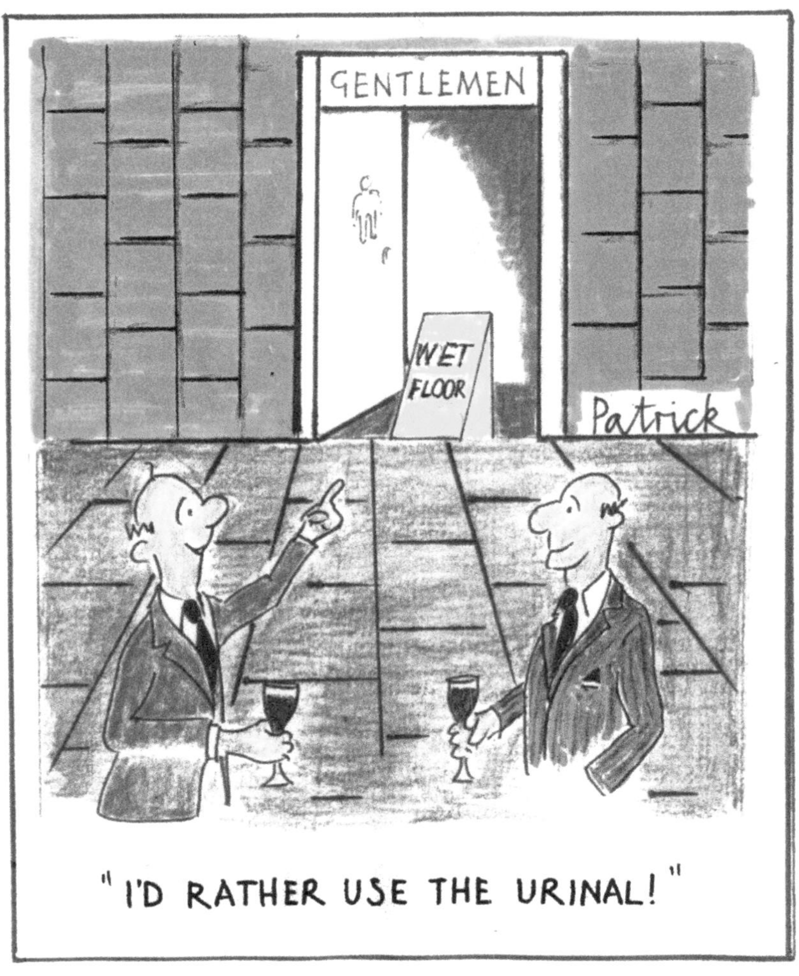
GENTLEMEN
WET FLOOR
Patrick

"I'D RATHER USE THE URINAL!"

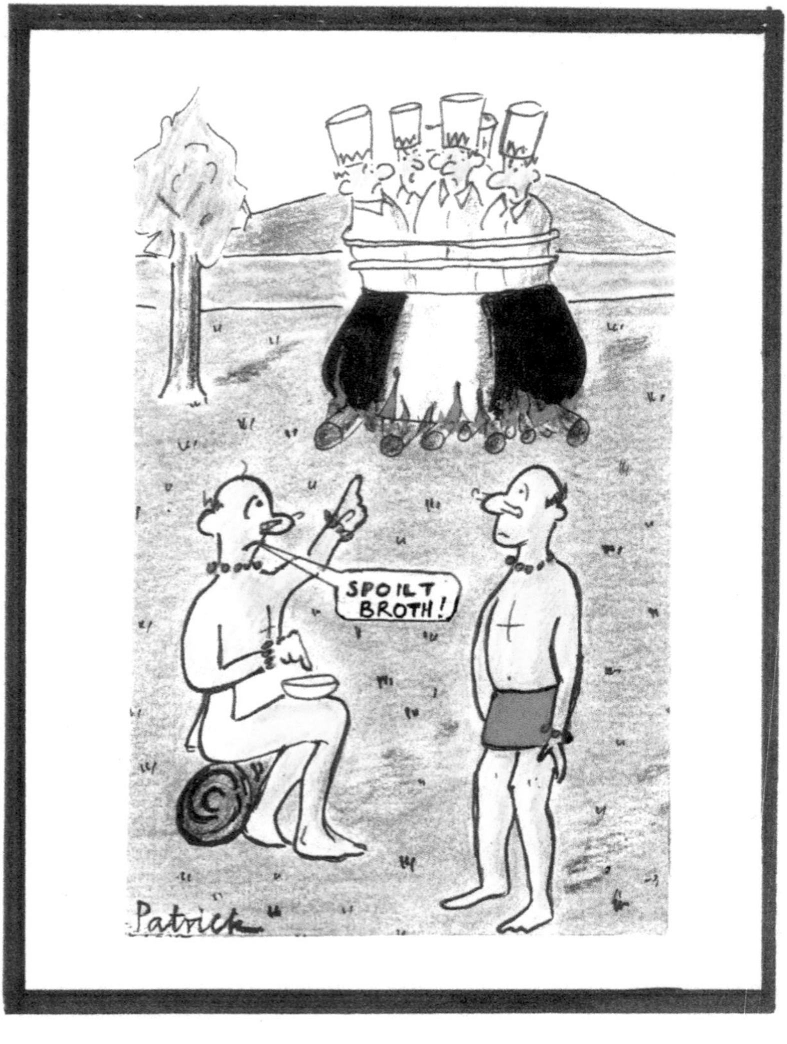
SPOILT BROTH!
Patrick

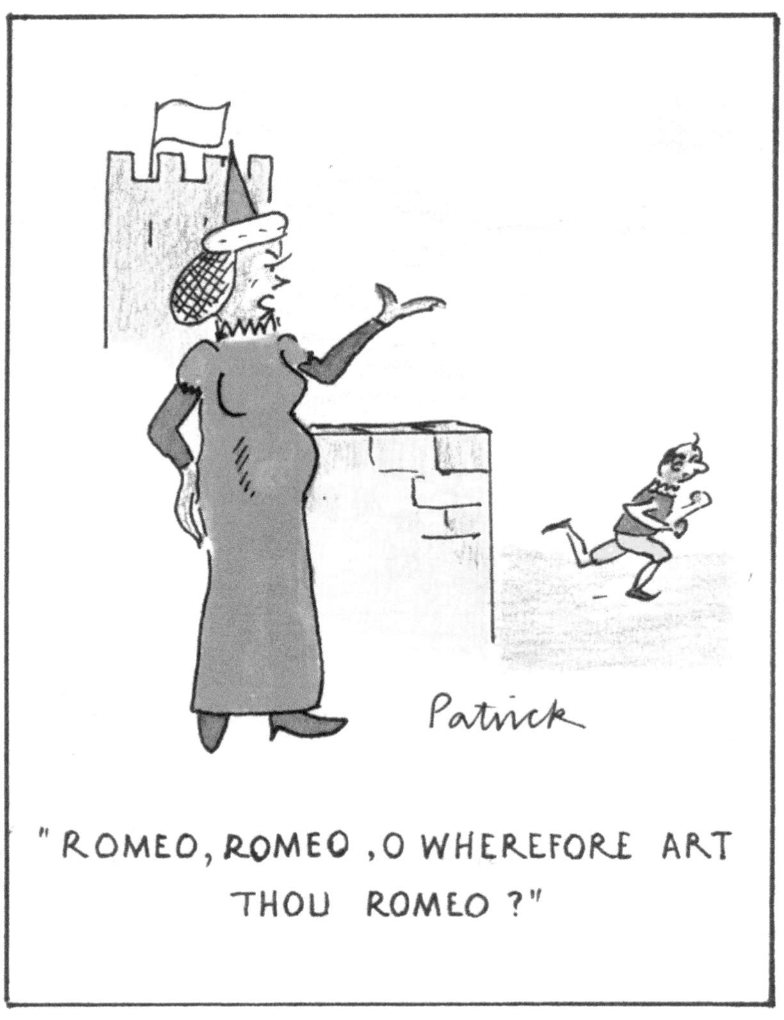
Patrick

"ROMEO, ROMEO, O WHEREFORE ART THOU ROMEO?"

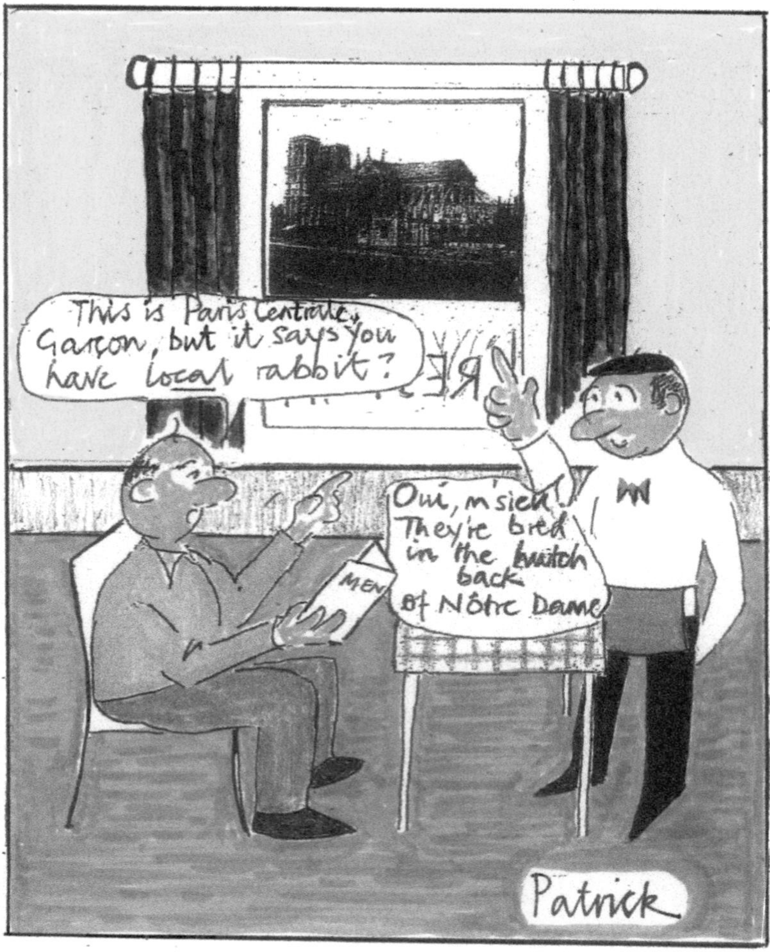
This is Paris Centrale, Garçon, but it says you have local rabbit?
Oui, m'sieu! They're bred in the hutch back of Nôtre Dame
MEN
Patrick

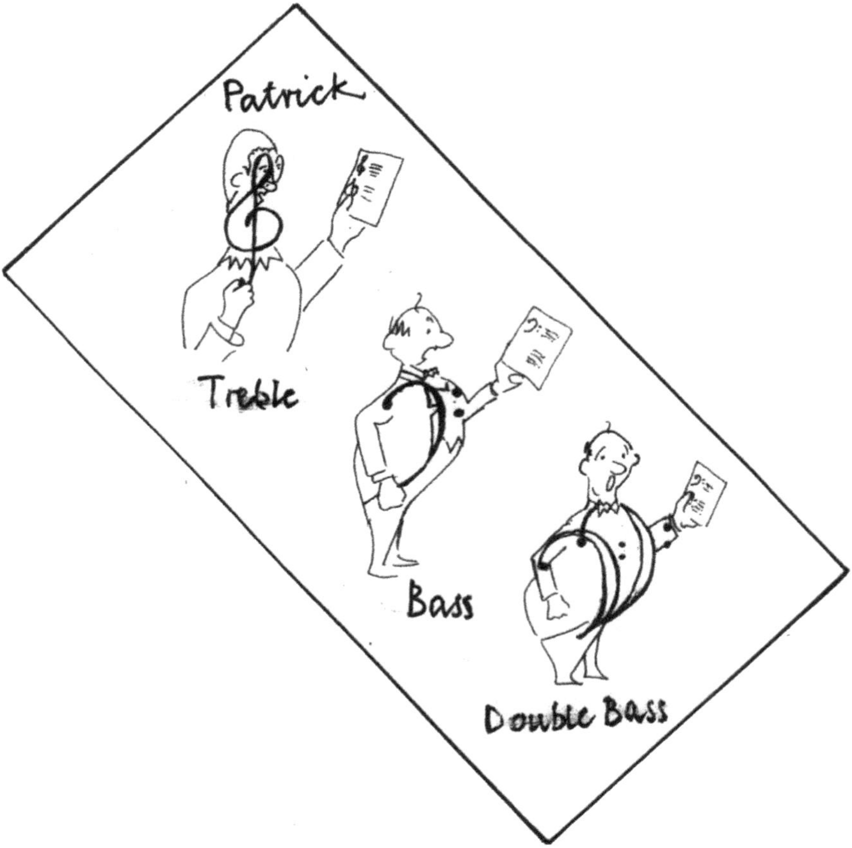
Patrick
Treble
Bass
Double Bass

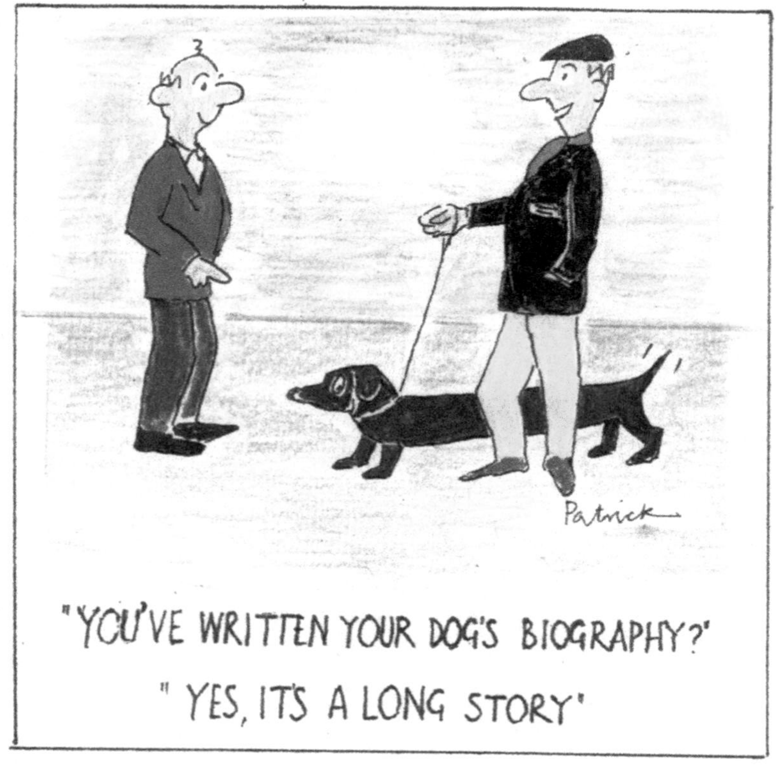
Patrick

"YOU'VE WRITTEN YOUR DOG'S BIOGRAPHY?'

" YES, IT'S A LONG STORY'

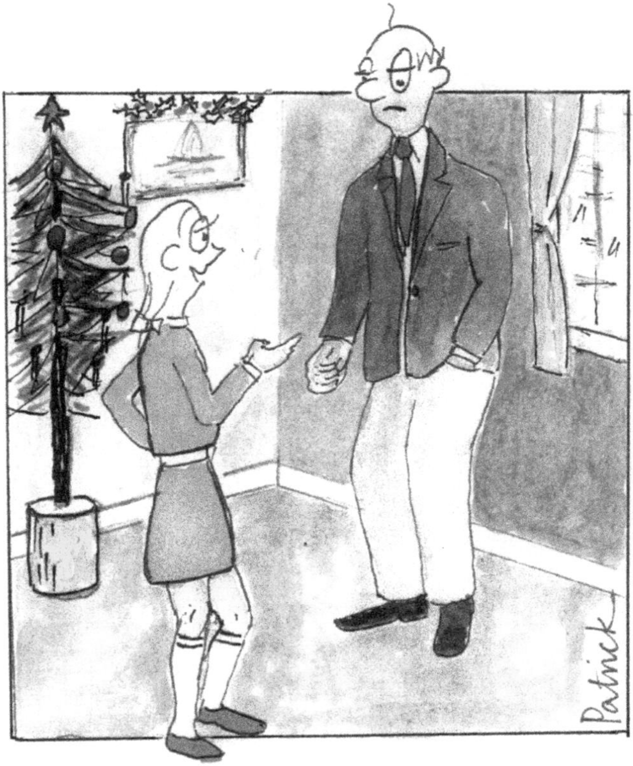
Patrick

"DADDY, MAY WE HAVE A DOG FOR XMAS ?"
"NO – WE'LL HAVE A TURKEY, LIKE EVERYONE ELSE!"

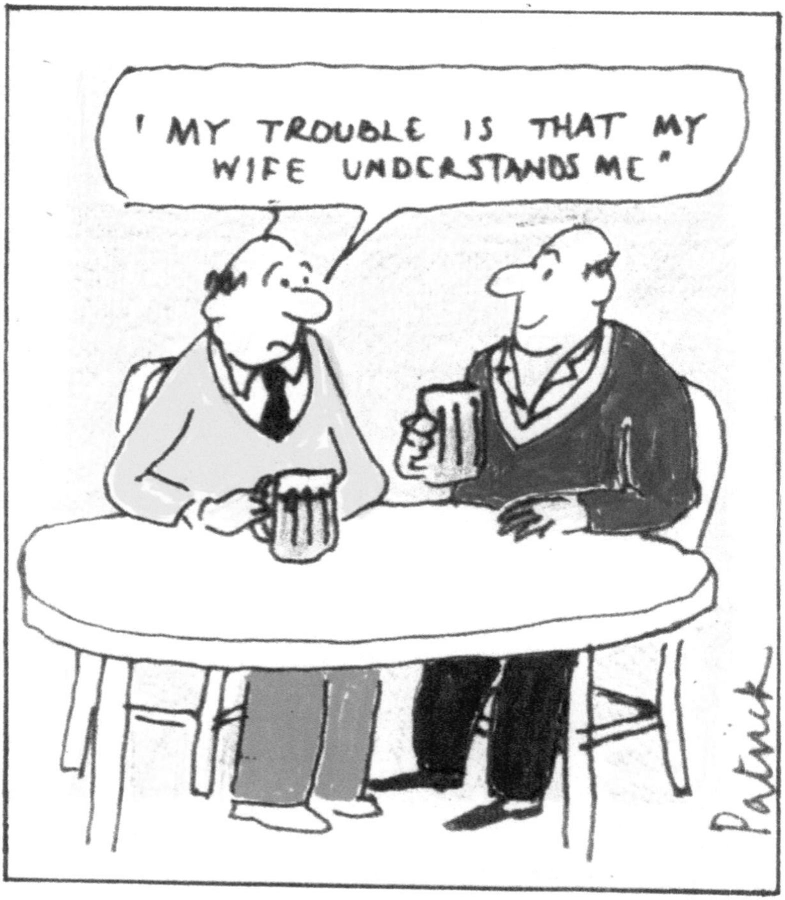
' MY TROUBLE IS THAT MY WIFE UNDERSTANDS ME"
Patrick

SWISS ARMY WIFE..

Patrick

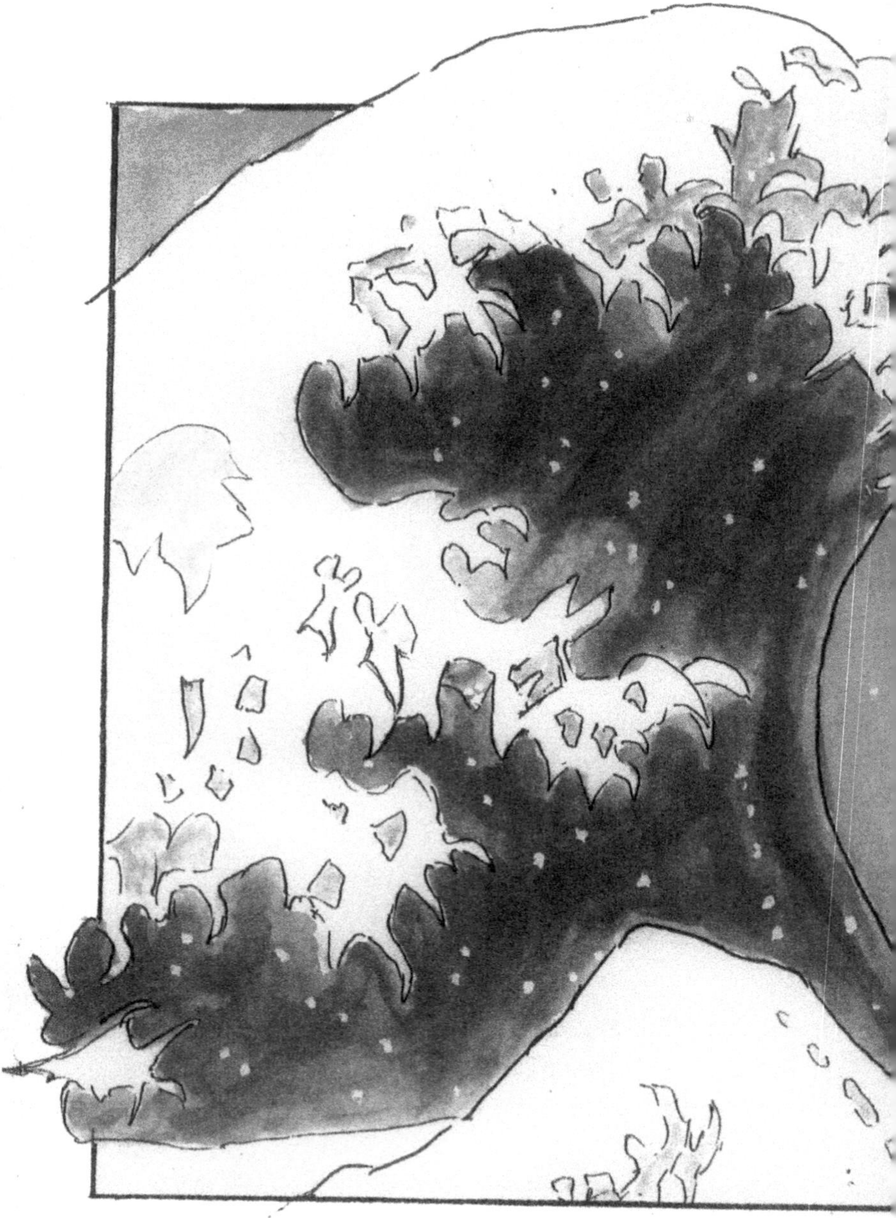

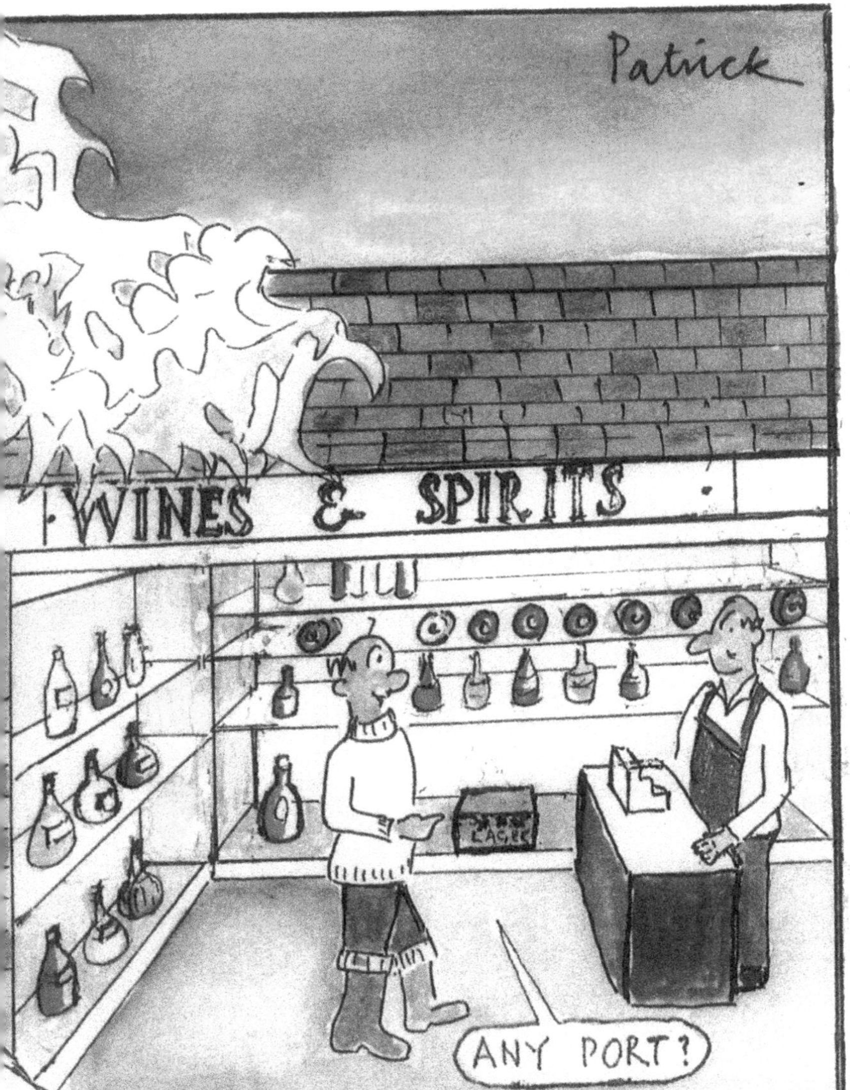
Patrick
WINES & SPIRITS
LAGER
ANY PORT?

Apologies to Hokusai

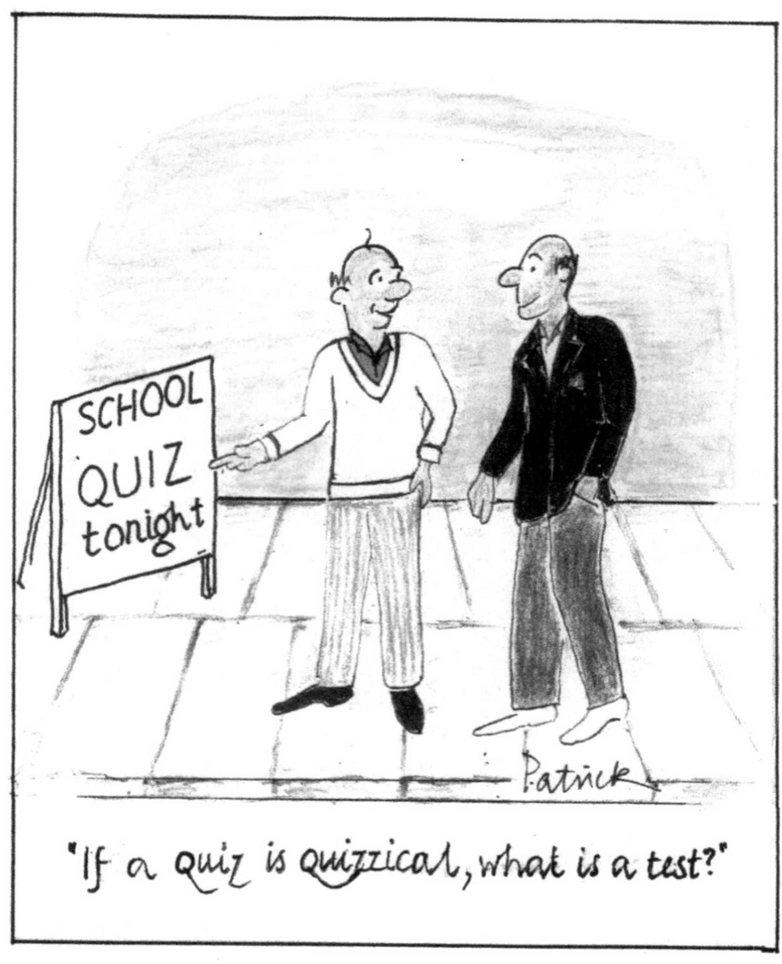
SCHOOL
QUIZ
tonight
Patrick

"If a quiz is quizzical, what is a test?"

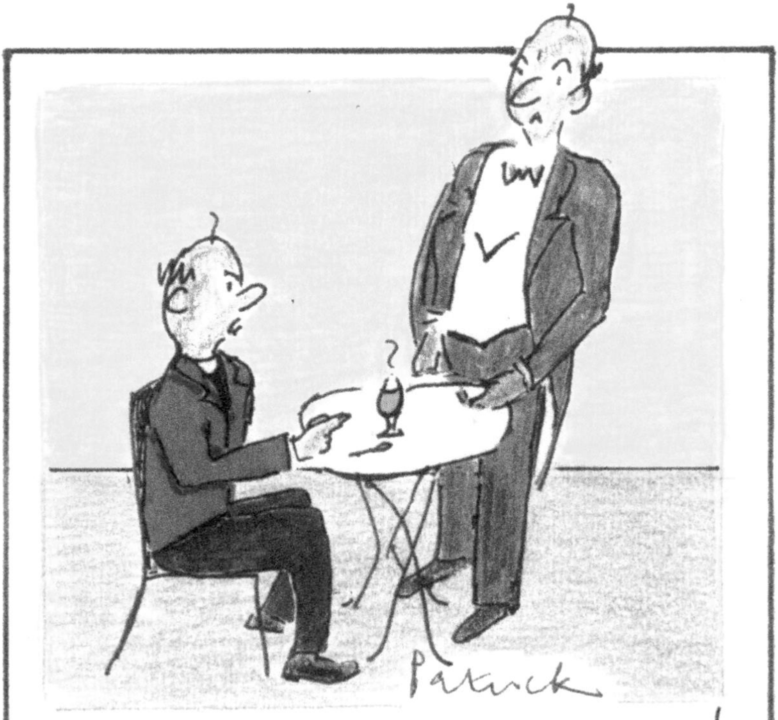
Patrick

"Waiter, this egg is bad!"
"Don't blame me, sir, I only laid the table."

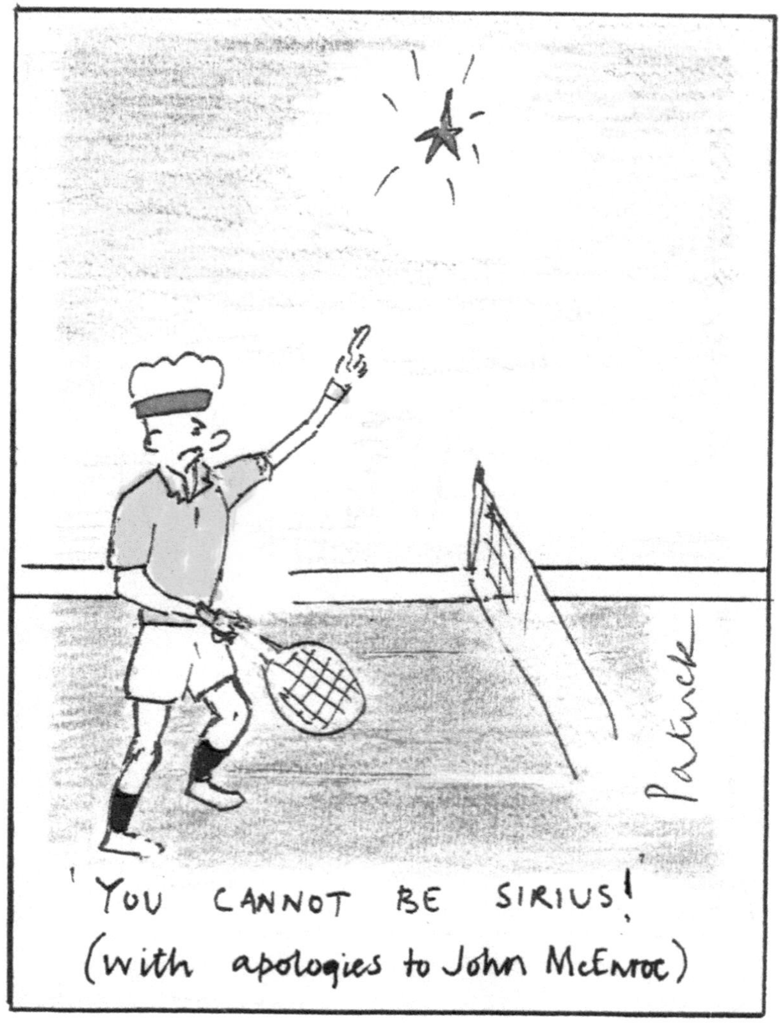
Patrick

'YOU CANNOT BE SIRIUS!'
(with apologies to John McEnroe)

"WHY DO THEY NEED A FENCE ROUND THE CEMETERY?
— PEOPLE ARE JUST DYING TO GET IN.."

Patrick

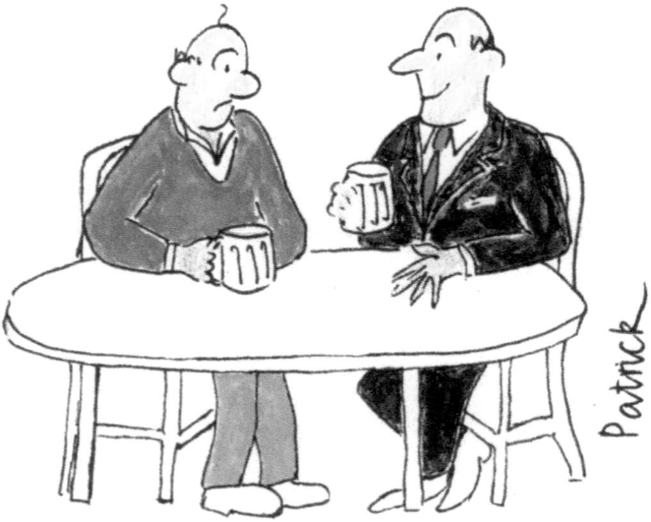
Patrick

"WHEN I CRITICISED MY WIFE'S JUDGEMENT, SHE AGREED & SAID 'LOOK WHO I MARRIED!'"

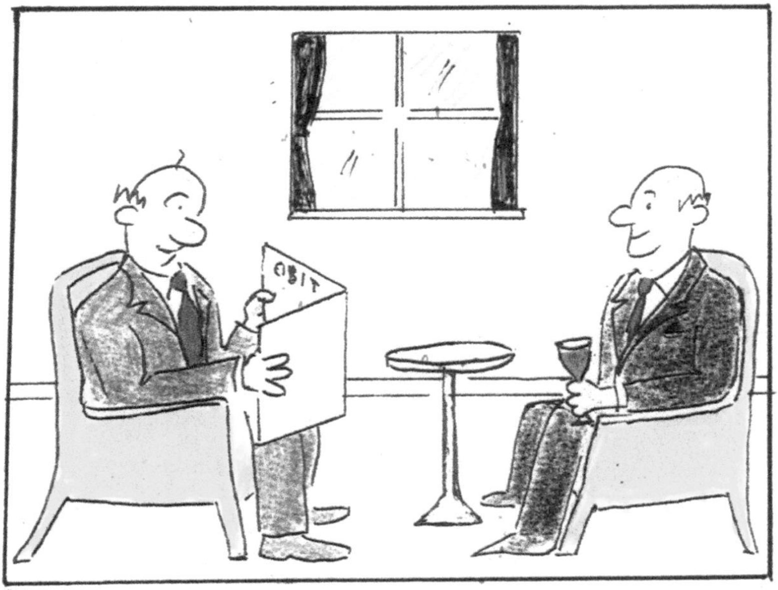
OBIT

"WHY DO PEOPLE ALWAYS DIE
IN ALPHABETICAL ORDER?"

Patrick

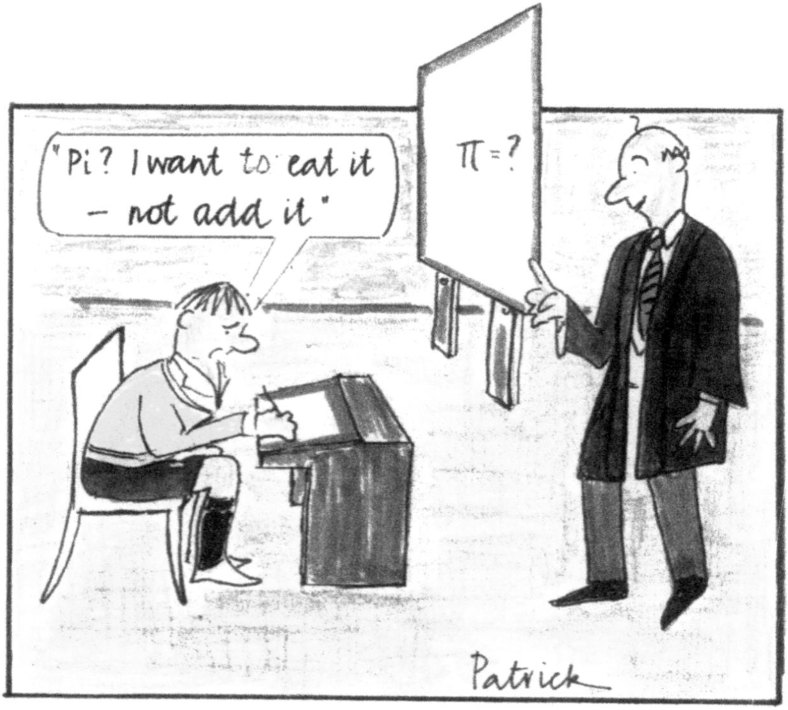
"Pi? I want to eat it – not add it"
π = ?
Patrick

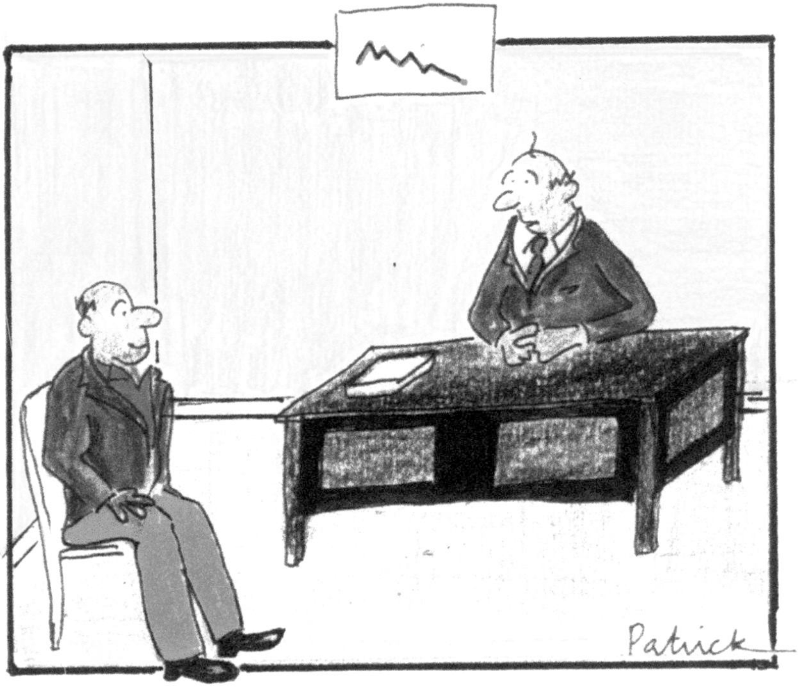
Patrick

"I KEEP PUSHING THE ENVELOPE, BUT IT'S STILL STATIONERY..."

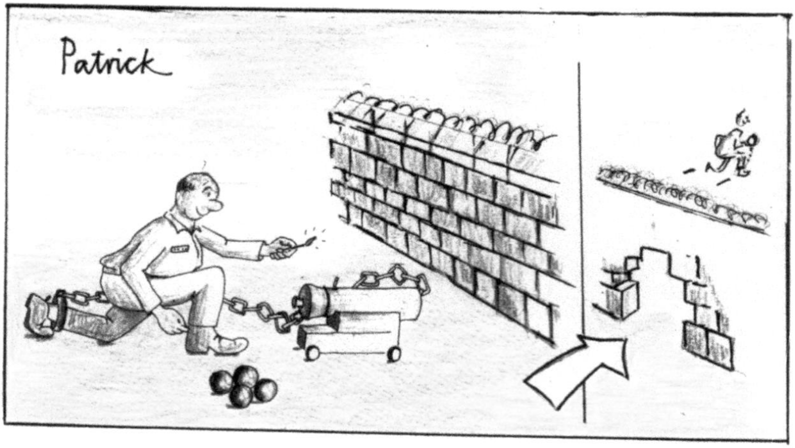
Patrick

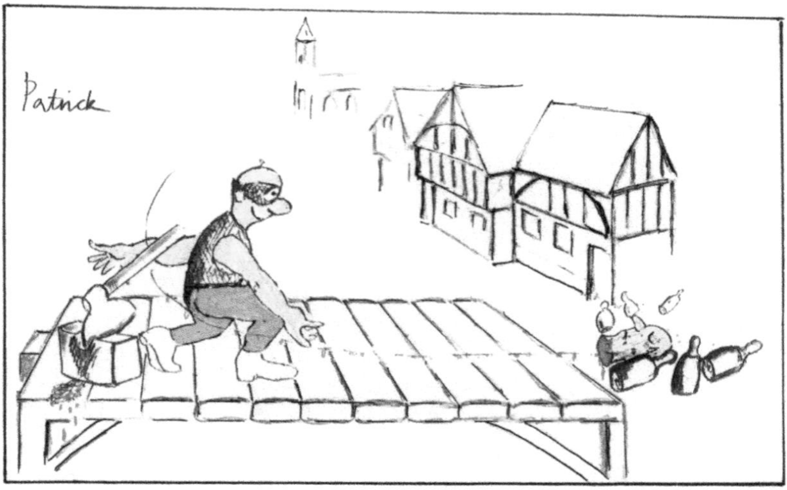
Patrick

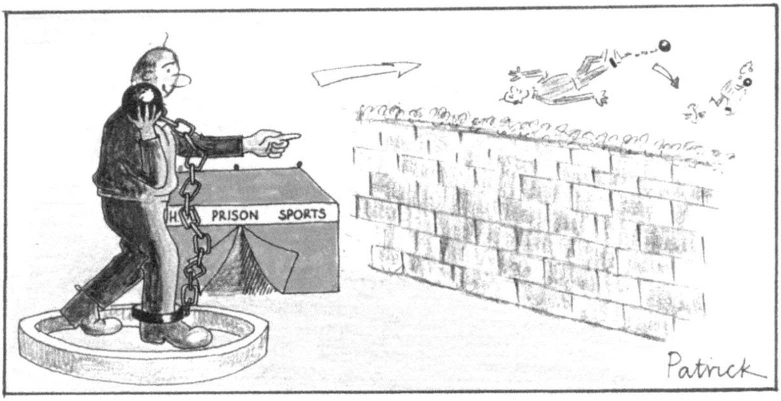
PRISON SPORTS
Patrick

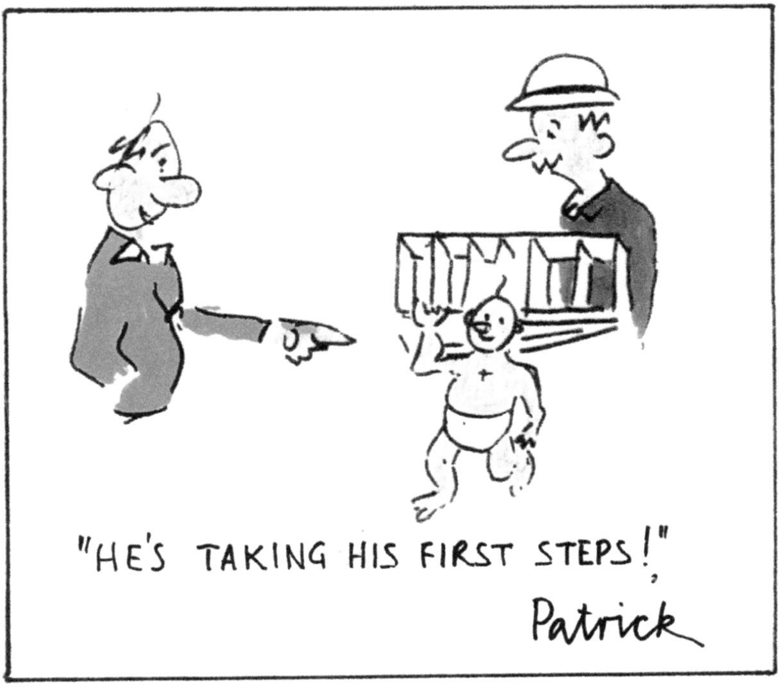
"HE'S TAKING HIS FIRST STEPS!"
Patrick

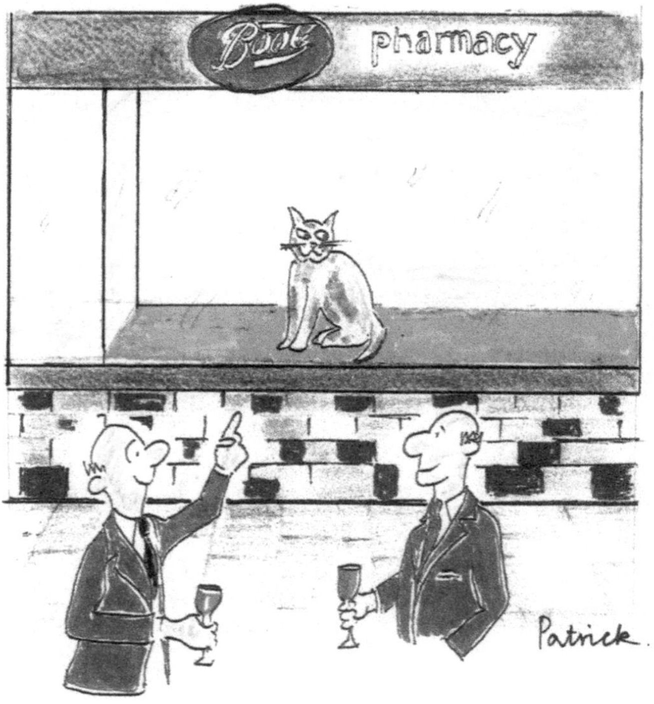
Boots
pharmacy
Patrick.

" ISN'T THAT A PANTOMIME ? "

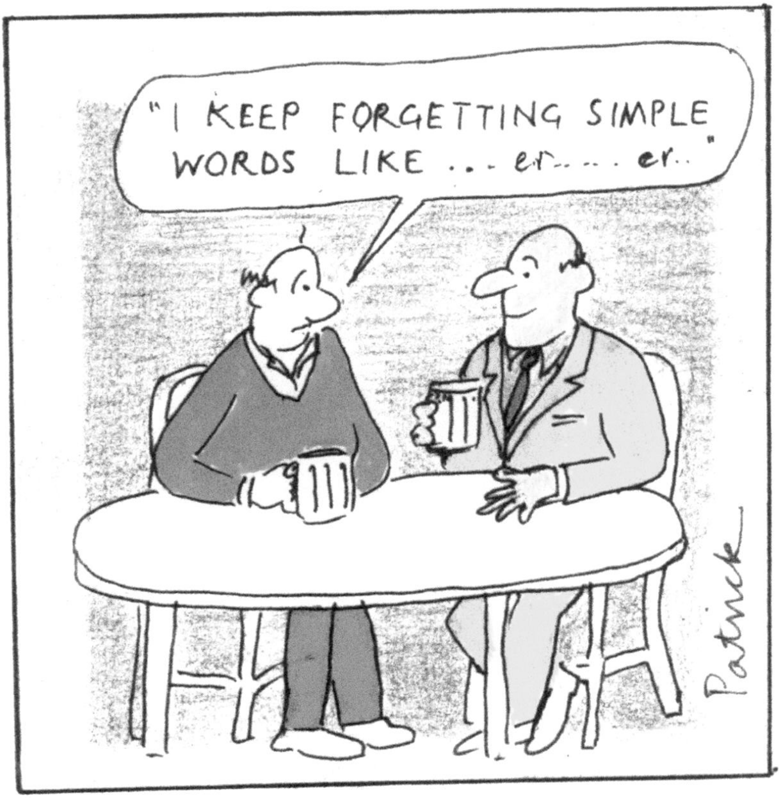
"I KEEP FORGETTING SIMPLE WORDS LIKE ... er.... er.."
Patrick

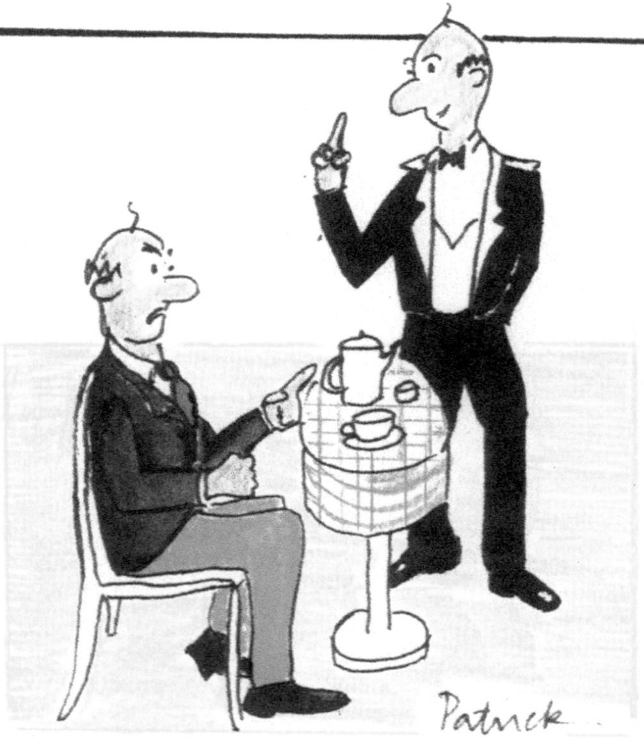
Patrick

"WAITER, THIS COFFEE TASTES LIKE MUD"
"YES SIR, IT'S JUST BEEN GROUND"

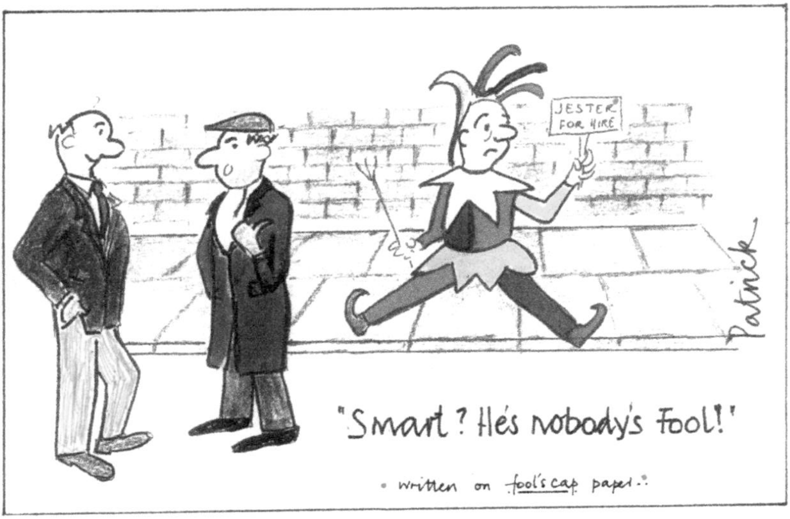
JESTER
FOR HIRE
Patrick

"Smart? He's nobody's Fool!"

• written on fool's cap paper •

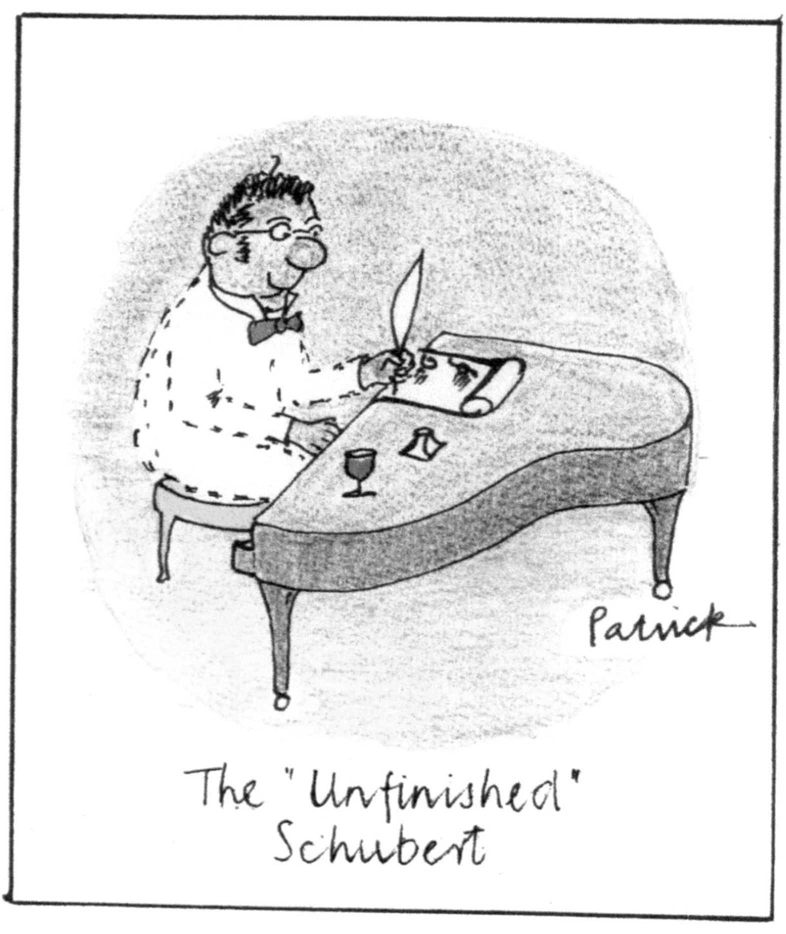
Patrick

The "Unfinished" Schubert

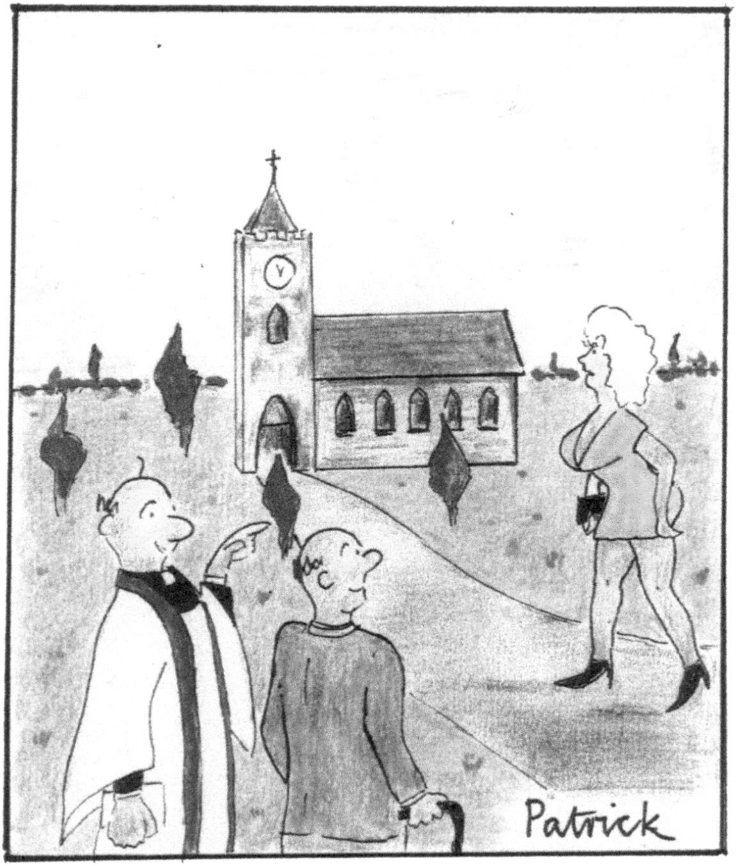
Patrick

SHE'S ONLY COMING BECAUSE SHE
~ THINKS A "HYMN" BOOK IS ~
~ A MALE ORDER CATALOGUE!

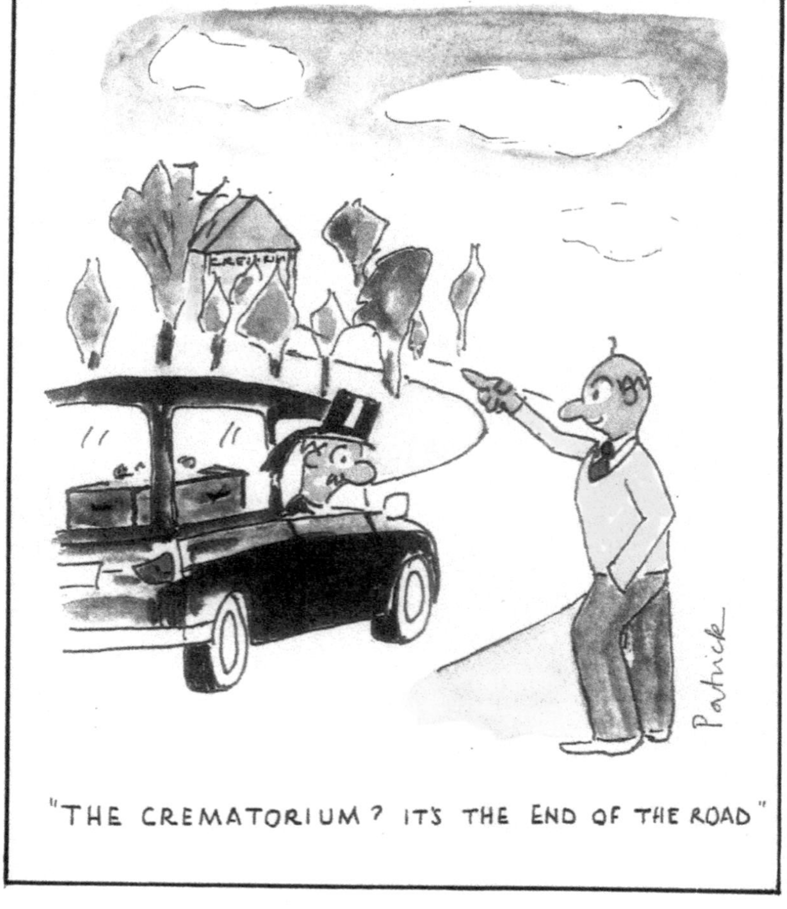
Patrick

"THE CREMATORIUM? IT'S THE END OF THE ROAD"

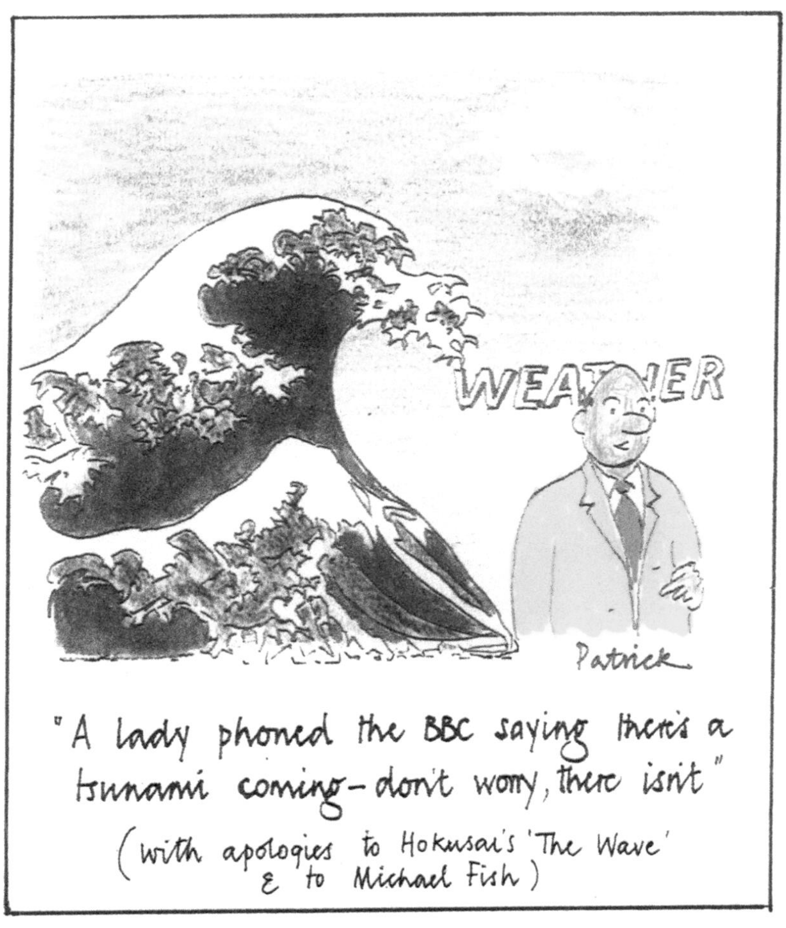
Patrick

"A lady phoned the BBC saying there's a tsunami coming – don't worry, there isn't"

(with apologies to Hokusai's 'The Wave' & to Michael Fish)

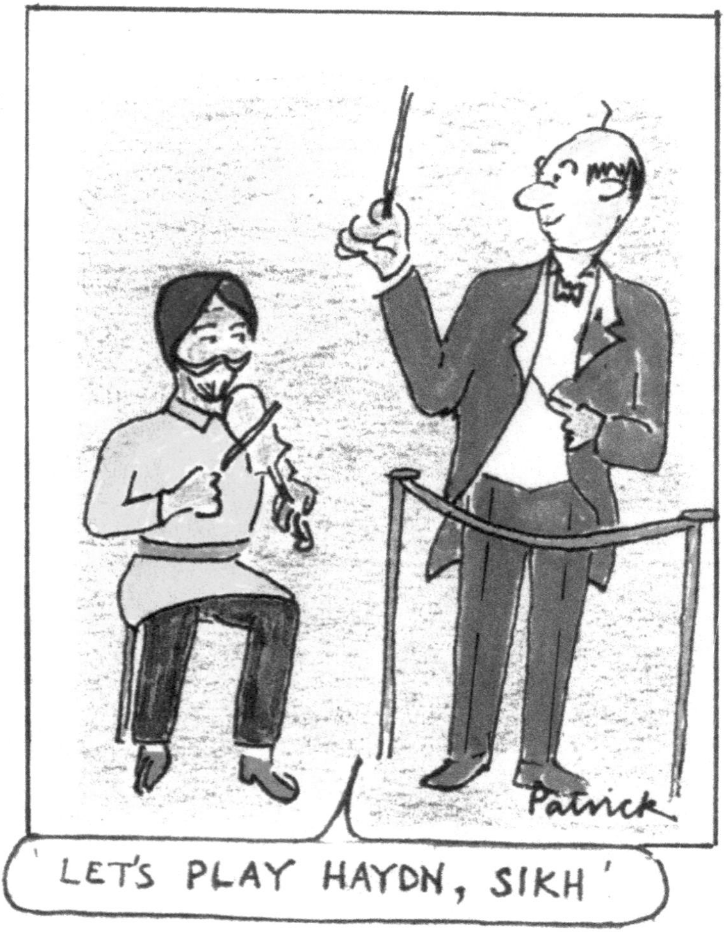
Patrick
'LET'S PLAY HAYDN, SIKH'

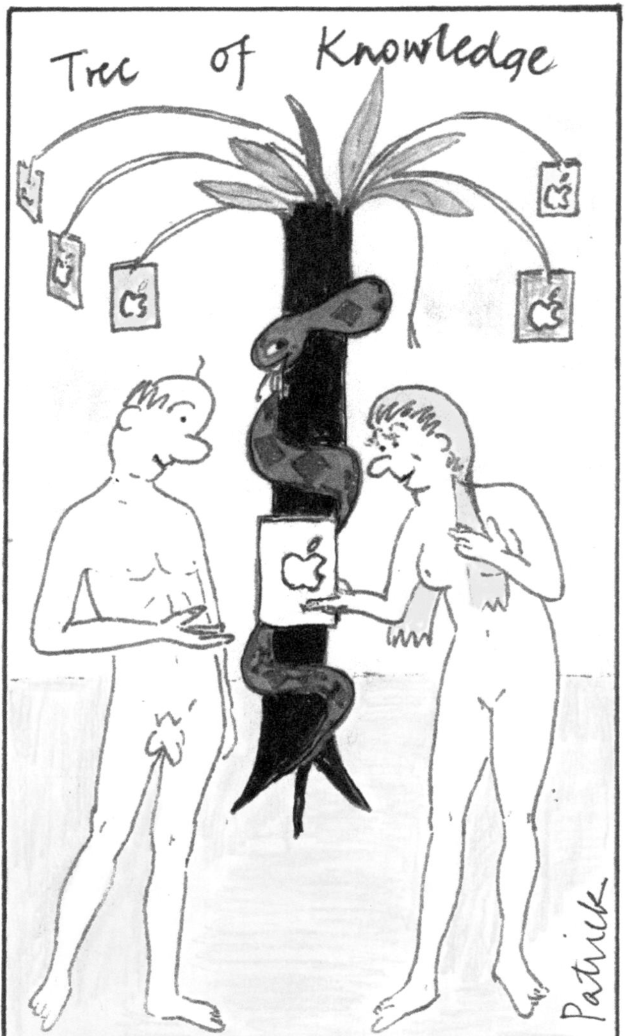
Tree of Knowledge
Patrick

Adam's Apple

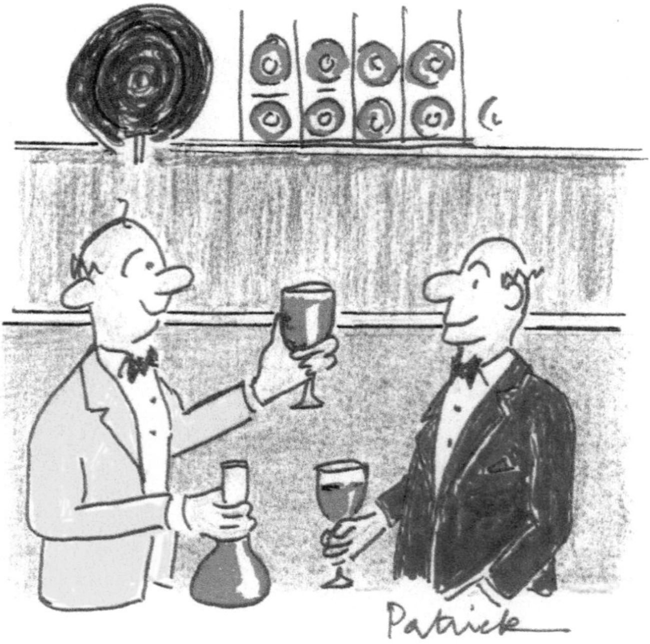
Patrick

"IT'S TRUE THAT WINE GETS BETTER WITH AGE – THE OLDER I GET, THE BETTER I LIKE IT!"

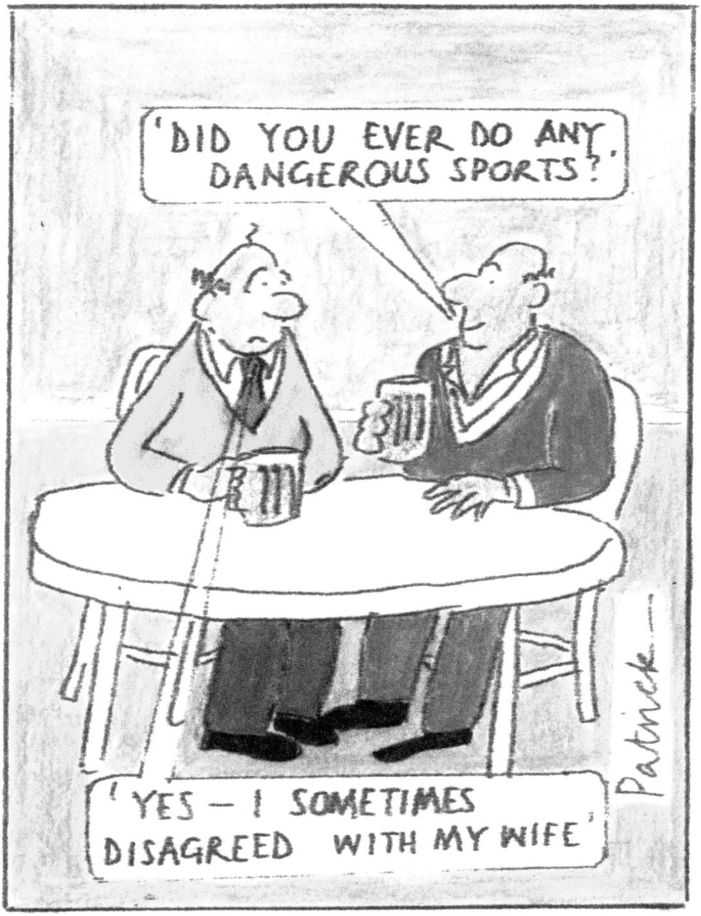
'DID YOU EVER DO ANY DANGEROUS SPORTS?'
'YES – I SOMETIMES DISAGREED WITH MY WIFE'
Patrick

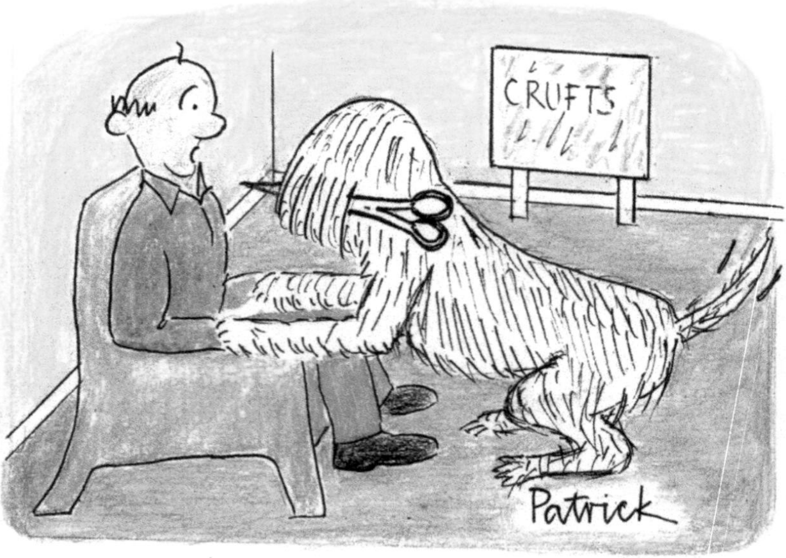
CRUFTS
Patrick

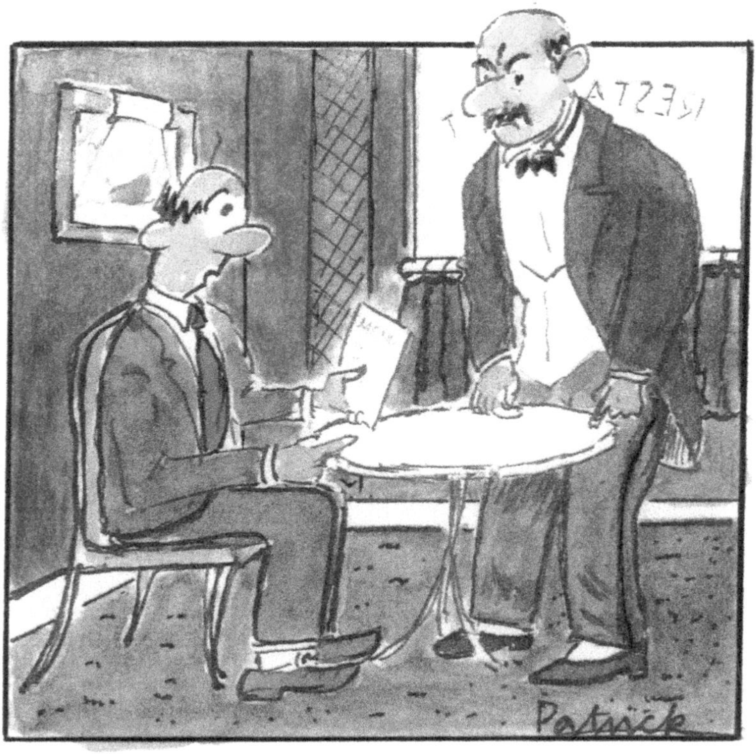
Patrick

'WAITER, DO YOU HAVE SPARE RIBS?'

'NO SIR, THIS IS A RESTAURANT, NOT THE GARDEN OF EDEN!

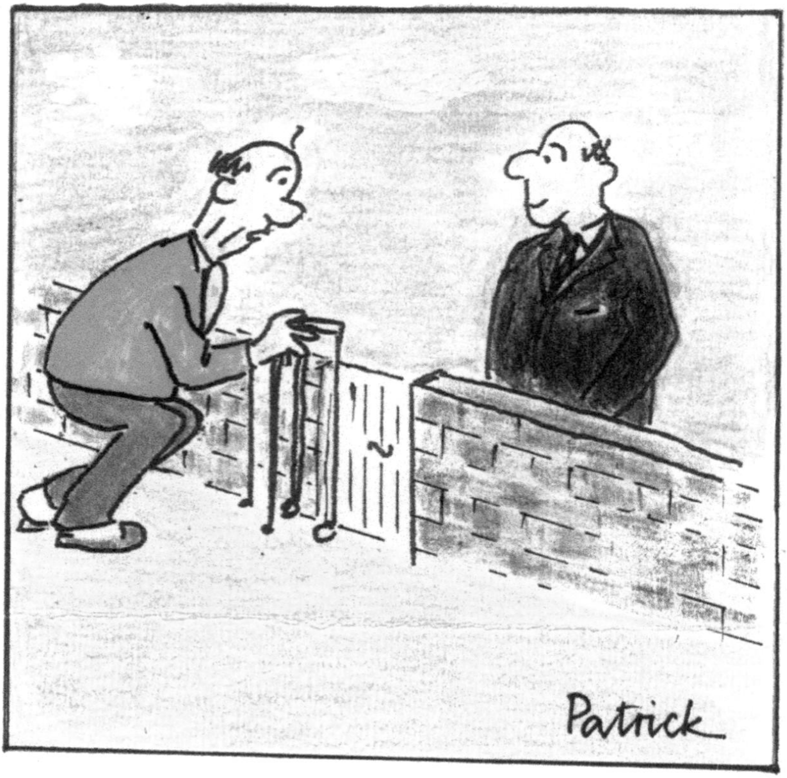
Patrick

"A PARTY ? NO THANKS – THESE DAYS ONLY MY BACK GOES OUT"

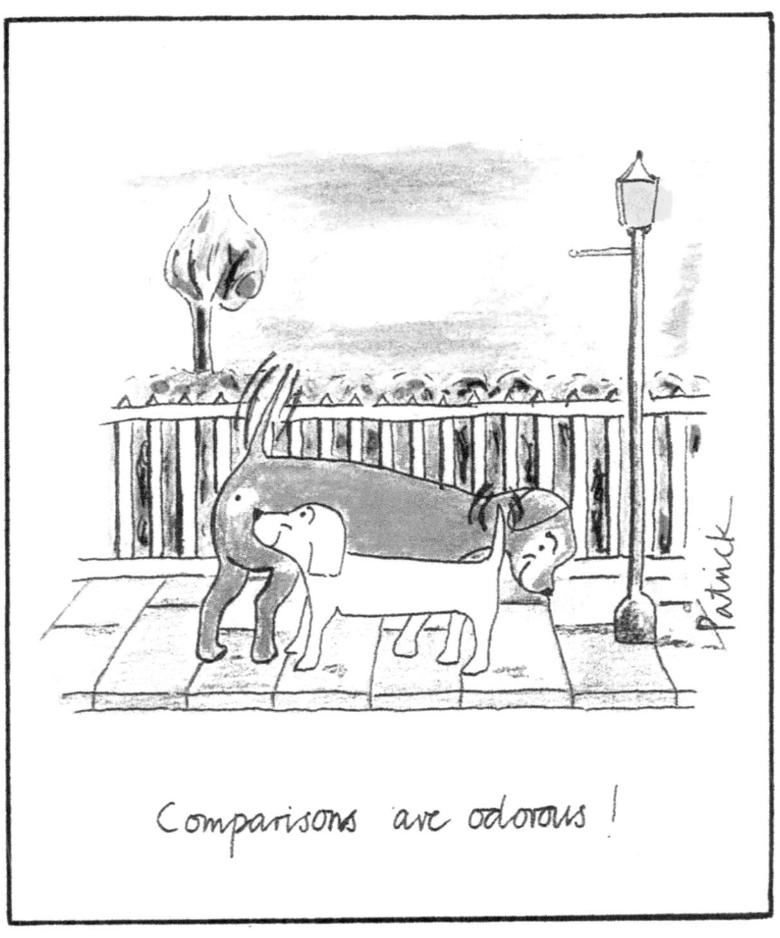
Patrick

Comparisons are odorous!

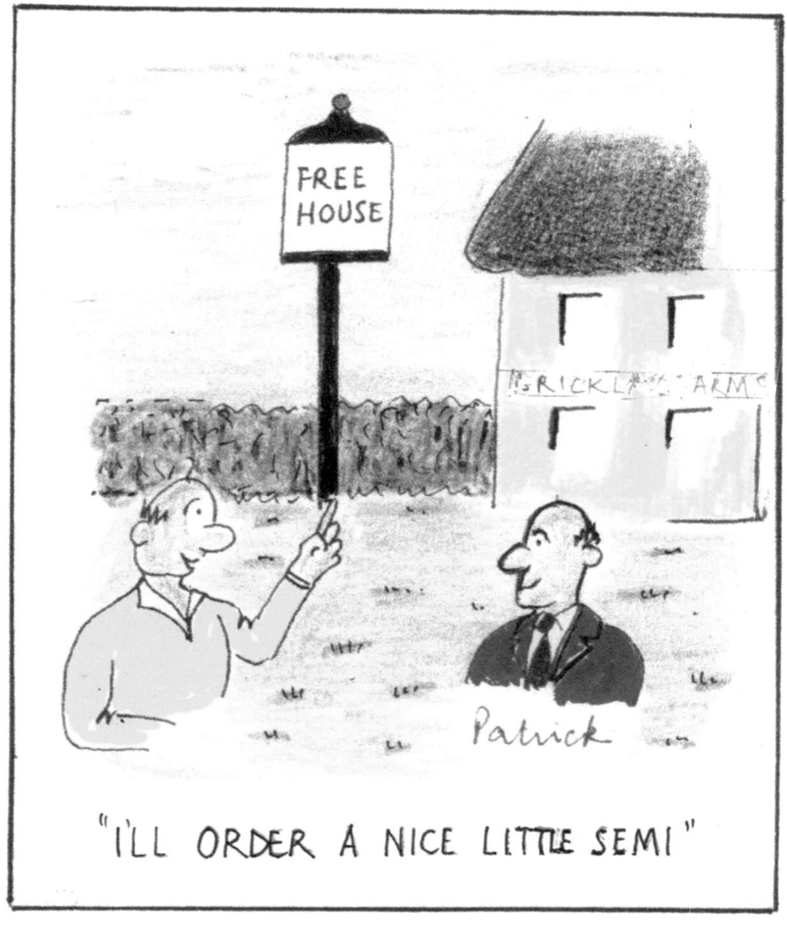
FREE
HOUSE
Patrick

"I'LL ORDER A NICE LITTLE SEMI"

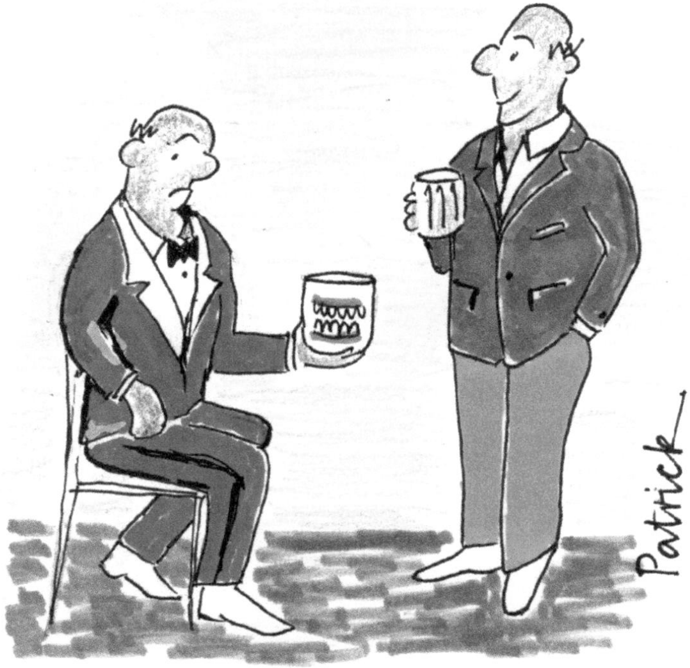
Patrick

I MISTOOK THE DENTIST FOR THE WINE BAR – AND ORDERED "APERATIF"

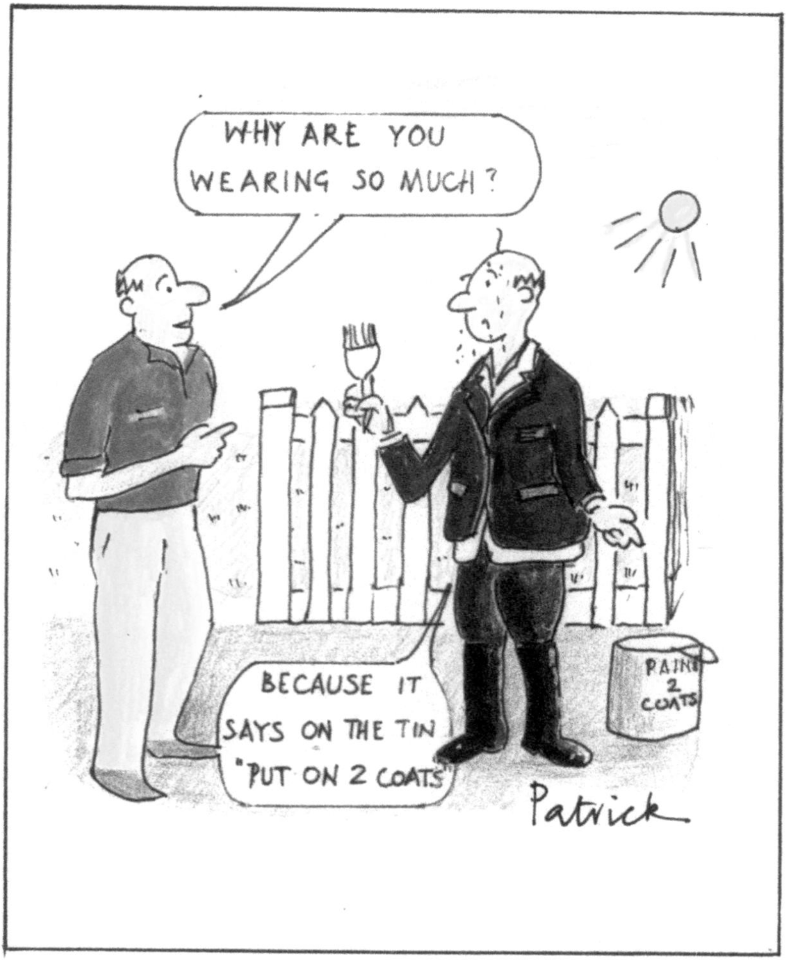
WHY ARE YOU WEARING SO MUCH?
BECAUSE IT SAYS ON THE TIN "PUT ON 2 COATS"
PAINT 2 COATS
Patrick

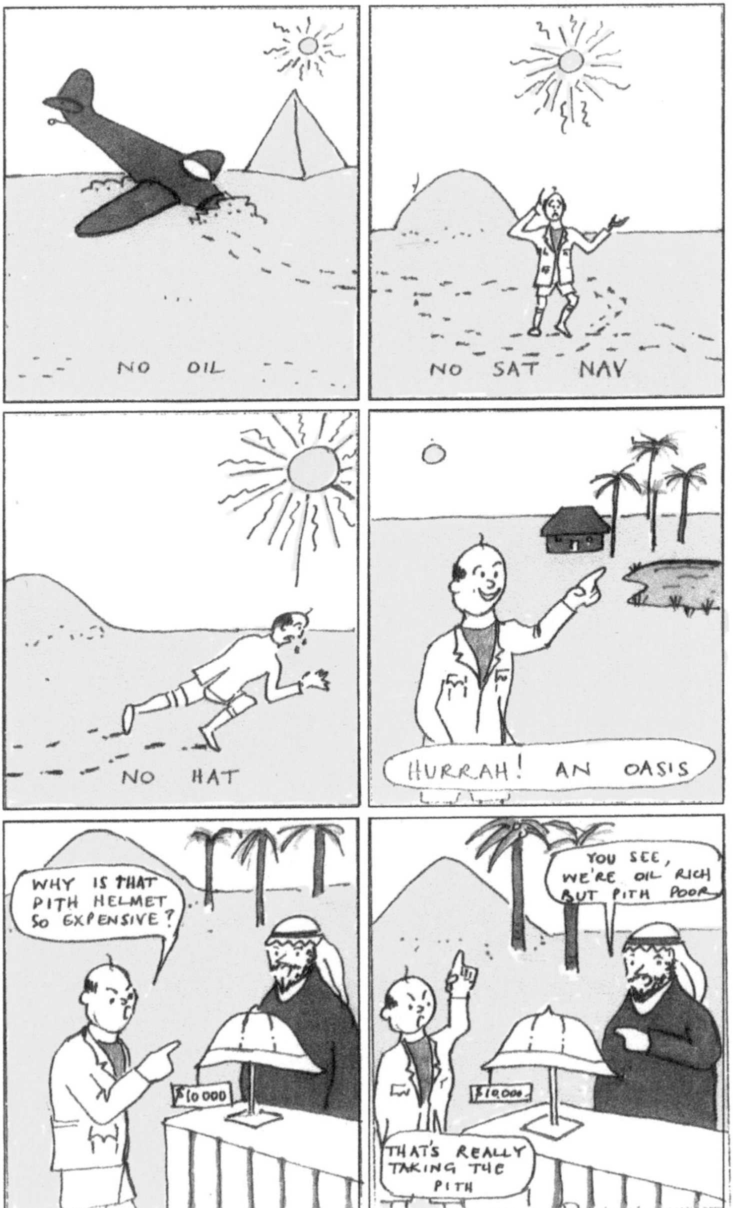
NO OIL
NO SAT NAV
NO HAT
HURRAH! AN OASIS
WHY IS THAT PITH HELMET SO EXPENSIVE?
$10 000
YOU SEE, WE'RE OIL RICH BUT PITH POOR
$10,000
THAT'S REALLY TAKING THE PITH
Patrick

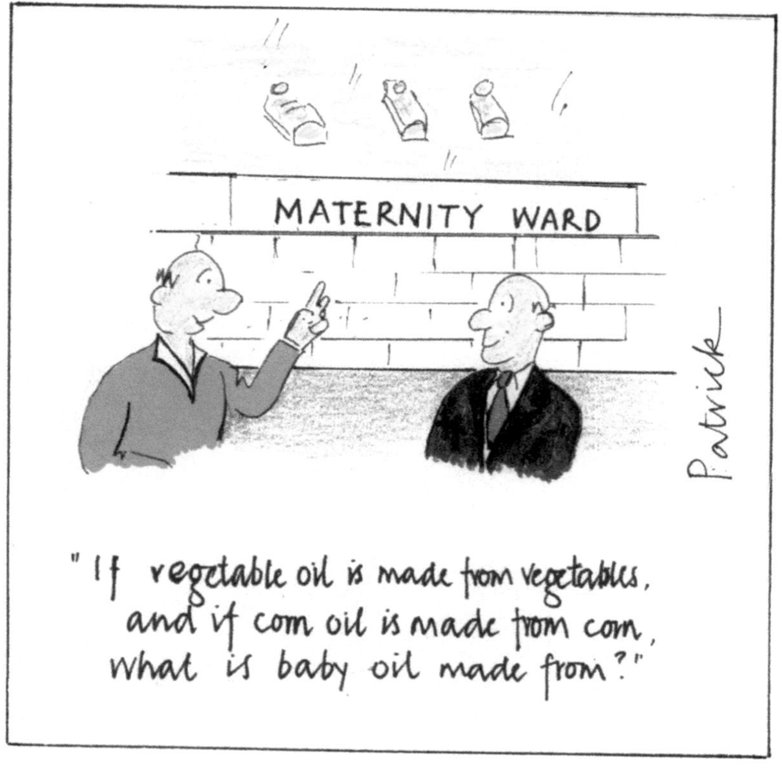
MATERNITY WARD
Patrick

"If vegetable oil is made from vegetables, and if corn oil is made from corn, what is baby oil made from?"

Patrick

'WHEN I ADVERTISED FOR A WIFE, I GOT
A HUNDRED LETTERS FROM MEN, SAYING
"HAVE MINE!"'

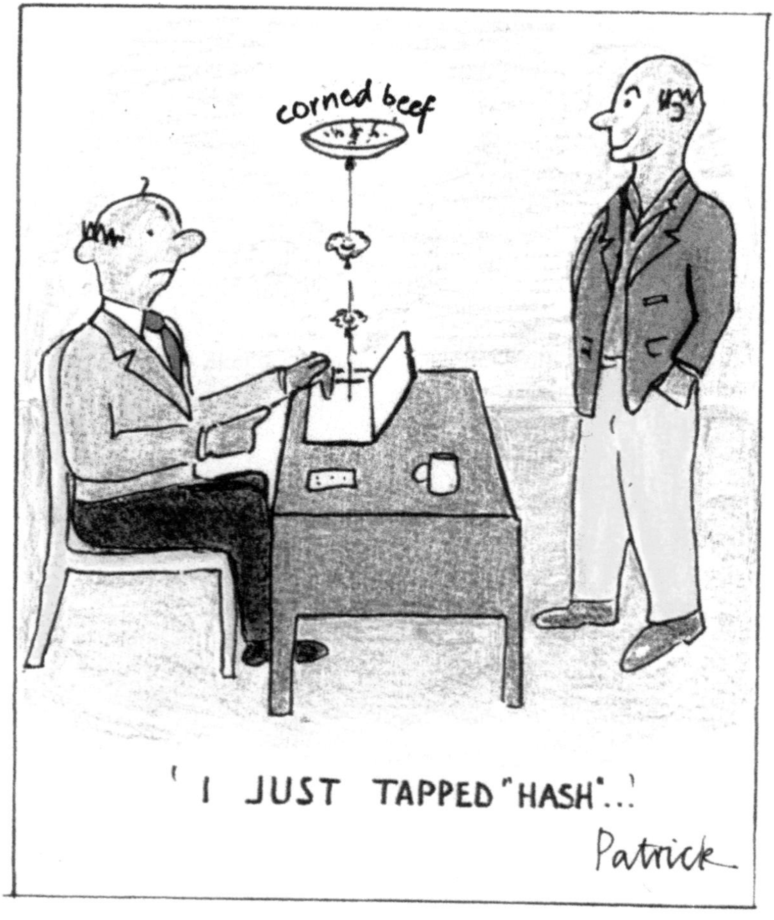
corned beef

'I JUST TAPPED "HASH"...'

Patrick

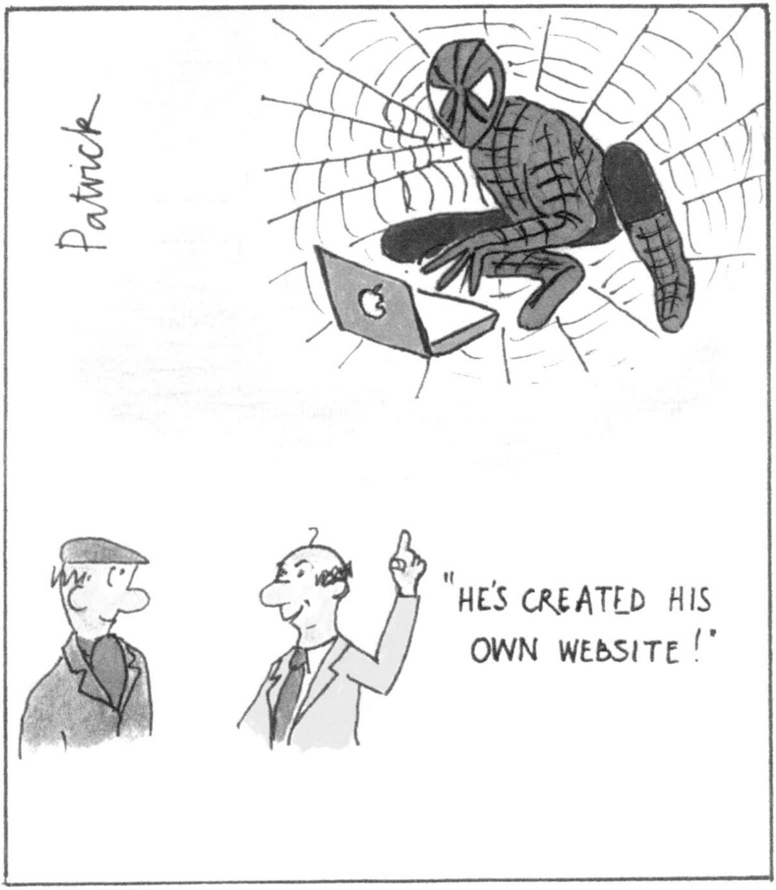
Patrick
"HE'S CREATED HIS OWN WEBSITE!"

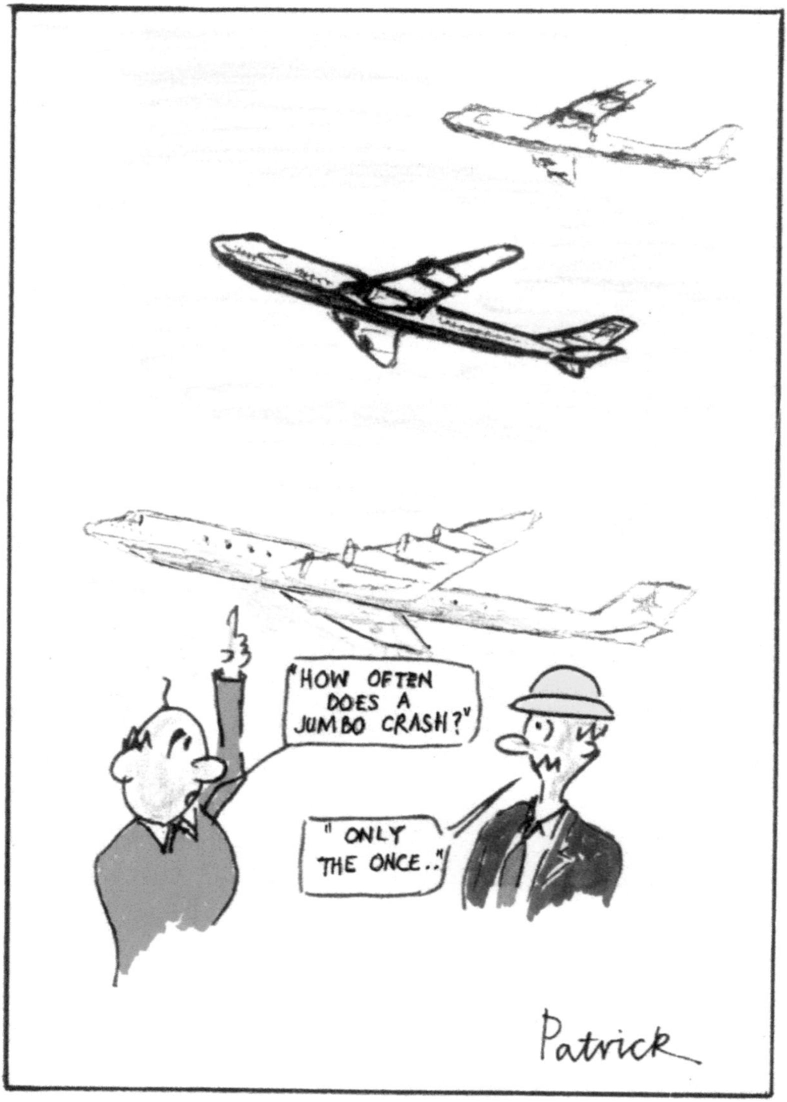
"HOW OFTEN DOES A JUMBO CRASH?"
"ONLY THE ONCE.."
Patrick

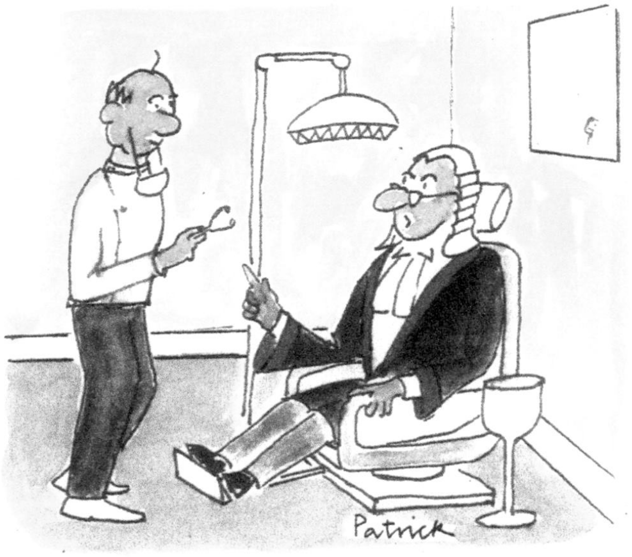
Patrick

"SWEAR TO EXTRACT THE TOOTH, THE WHOLE TOOTH AND NOTHING BUT THE TOOTH"

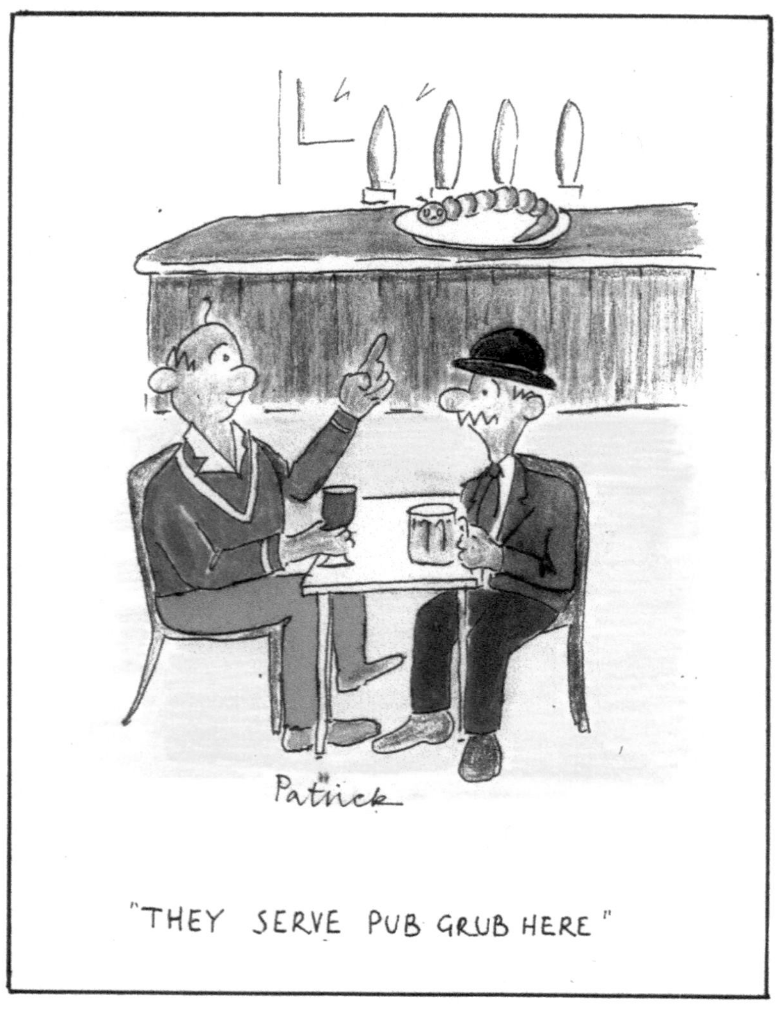
Patrick

"THEY SERVE PUB GRUB HERE"

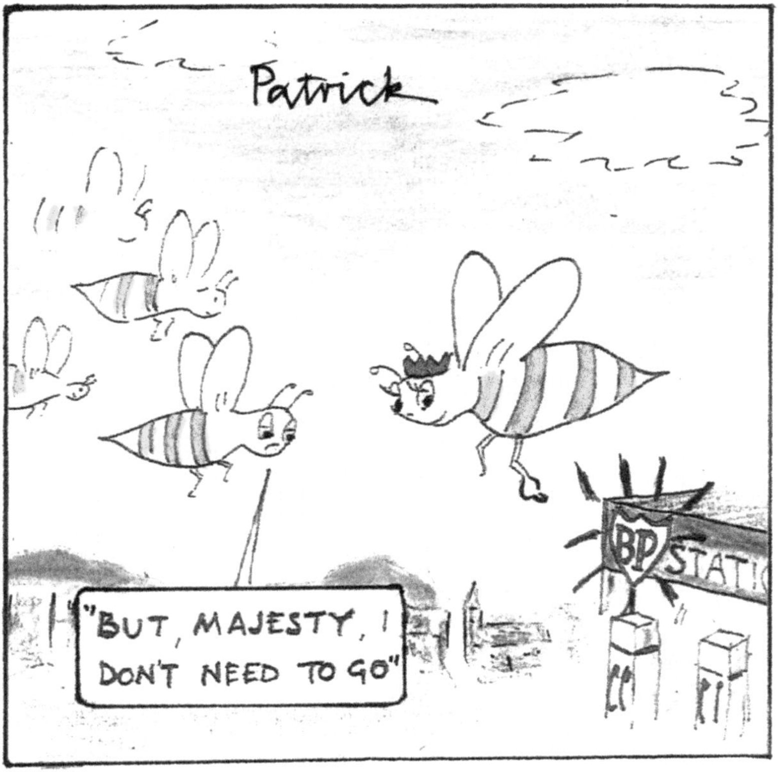
Patrick
"BUT, MAJESTY, I DON'T NEED TO GO"
BP
STATI

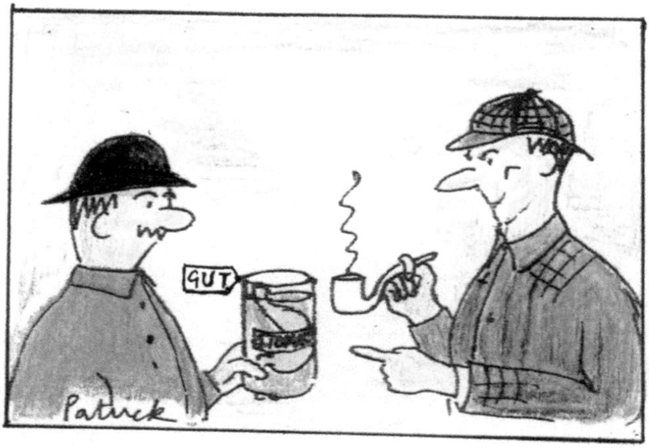
GUT
Patrick

"IT'S ALIMENTARY, MY DEAR WATSON..."

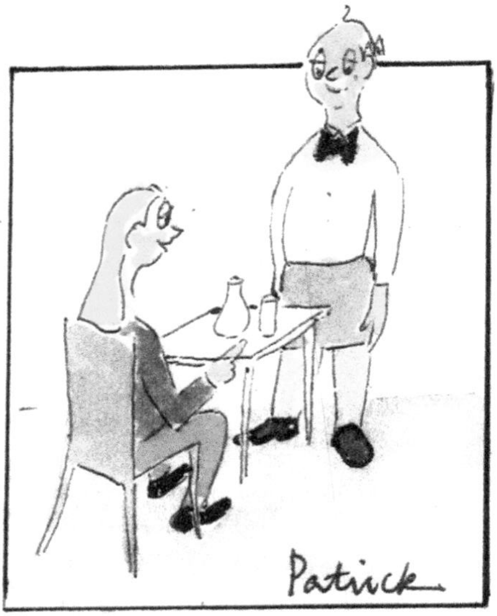
Patrick

"Waiter, is this water fit to drink?"

"Oh, yes. It's been passed personally by senior management."

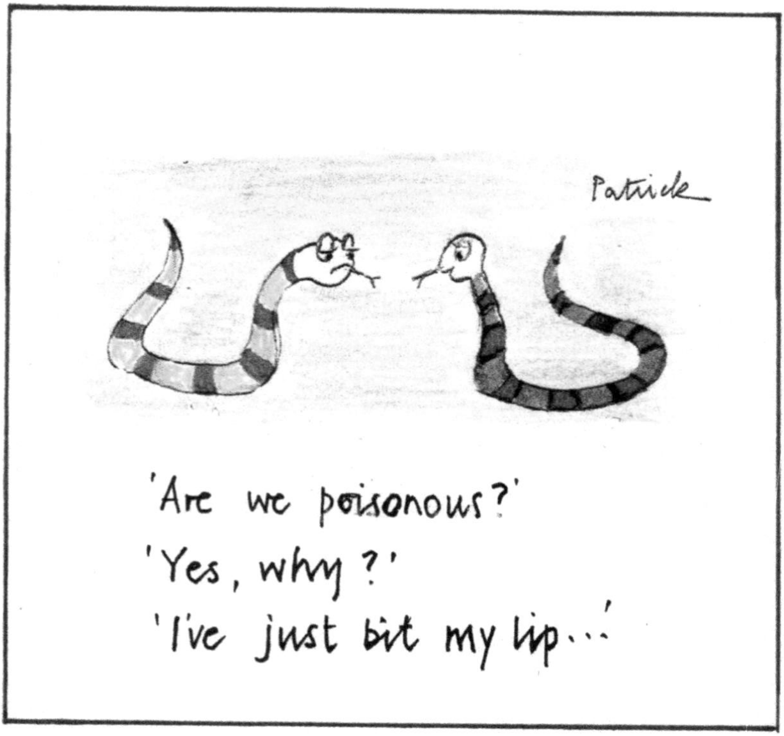
Patrick
'Are we poisonous?'
'Yes, why?'
'I've just bit my lip...'

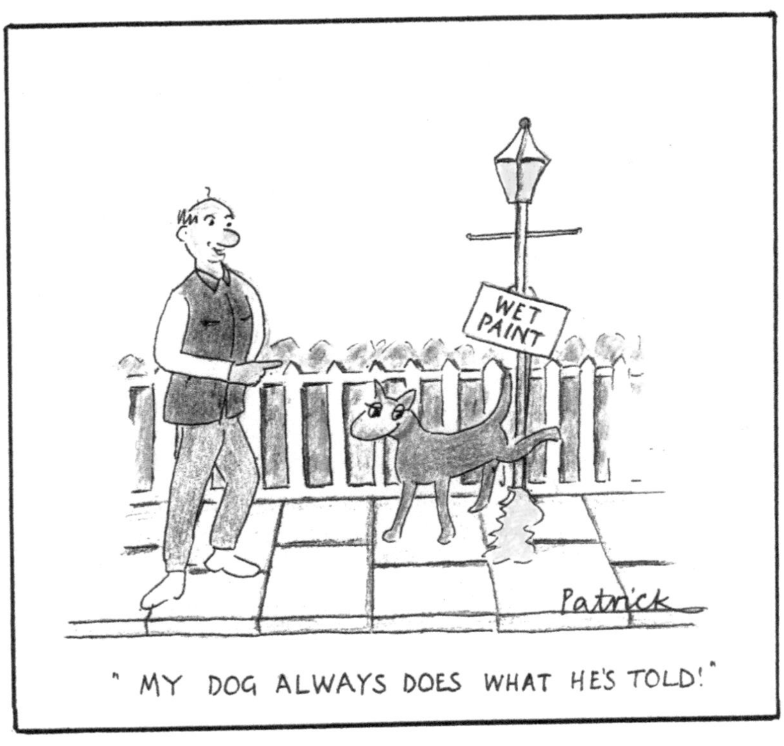
WET PAINT
Patrick

" MY DOG ALWAYS DOES WHAT HE'S TOLD! "

Patrick Holden

Lightning Source UK Ltd.
Milton Keynes UK
UKHW020822111219
355121UK00002B/10/P